THE PARADOX OF

CHRISTIANITY

TRUTH THAT MAGNIFIES THE LIES

BY GARY WENDELL STANFIELD SR.

Studies done by Gary Wendell Stanfield

All poems written by Gary W. Stanfield

I use the scriptures to prove things first, then use history along with the scriptures to prove other studies along with maps to help better your understanding.

DEDICATION

I dedicate this book to my family who have been brainwashed into Christianity, just as I was, and like the majority of the world's population has been. It was handed down through their parents, as it was by their parents—a generational deceit—because no one would believe that their parents would lie to them. This is a generational curse: believing what they were taught as truth without questioning it. I did, and I have done all the research and studying for you. I have not uncovered all the lies and deceit, and I never will. That is why Moses and Elijah must come and teach the whole truth, with salvation available for everyone, alive at that time.

All you must do is read my books to gain the true knowledge to free yourself from that deceit and find the true salvation that is coming again. Everything is proven by scripture. May these books open your mind to the Satanic deceit you are in. Your brother, father, uncle, grandfather, or whatever I may be to you—may you find the truth and hold to it when it is given once more. These books will prepare you for it, so you know what to look for.

With love,

Gary W. Stanfield

I need to tell a story that I heard years ago. A man was invited to dinner at a friend's house and noticed that she used a small pan to cook her chicken in. He asked her why. She said, "I don't know; it's the same size pan my mother used. Go ask her."

So, he did. Her mother told him to go ask her mother where she learned it from. The man went and asked her mother, and she said, "That was the only pan I had to fry chicken in."

That is like Christianity—or any other world religion—passed down without anyone ever asking why.

PREFACE

This book is a treasure trove of studies uncovering the truth behind the brainwashing perpetuated by Christian lies. It is a valuable resource for learning truths not taught within Christianity and for guiding you onto the path of salvation. Once Yahweh fills a person with His Spirit, which grants salvation, there is no such thing as backsliding. His Spirit is poured out again, and the truth is taught before the Tribulation Period and His return at the end of it.

No one can be judged without hearing the whole truth and having the opportunity for salvation. Yahweh has made a way for everyone to hear the full truth, whether they died after Constantine's 11th Roman Emperor persecution, never having heard the truth with salvation available, up to the Papacy's 7-Year Peace Plan. Those still alive during the Peace Plan will also have the opportunity at that time.

In the meantime, you can begin to distance yourself from Christianity and stop using pagan names that keep people far from salvation. Names like Jesus, Christ, Lord, God, and Amen, among others used in Christian scriptures, distort the truth. These pagan names perpetuate lies, and it makes me cringe to hear them being used.

Through this book, you will discover that, despite what was done to Yahweh's Word, enough truth remains for people to find their way to Him and His salvation. However, salvation is not available to anyone today, dating back to Constantine's time. Only through Yahweh's love and mercy does He desire all men to receive salvation, though the scriptures make it clear this will not happen due to individual choice.

In this book, you will learn His true birth-given name and the actual city where He was born, which is not the one traditionally claimed. You will uncover the truth about the real City of David, which is not what is often passed off as such. Additionally, you will learn why tithing is not applicable today, the deceit behind the 10 Commandments Christianity teaches as true, and many other truths too numerous to mention here.

This book should challenge your way of thinking about the things you were taught to believe as true. I continue to learn more every day, which inspires me to keep studying. I hope this book will inspire you to do the same by testing and proving all things.

Table of Contents

CHAPTER 1

A. THE NAME IMMANUEL AS THE BIRTH GIVEN NAME:

This STUDY is a good study to start this book off with. Immanuel was the birth-given name that people knew him by for tax purposes and everyday living.

Matthew 13:55-56

[55.] **Is not this the carpenter's son? Is not his mother called Mariam? And his brethren, Jacob, and Joseph, and Simon, and Judah?**

[56.] **And his sisters, are they not all with us?** Whence then hath this man all these things?

Mark 6:3

Is not this the carpenter, the son of Mariam, the brother of Jacob, and Joseph? And are not his sisters here with us? And they were offended at him.

Jacob, Joseph, Judah, and Simon, the names of his brothers, are all Hebrew names, and Immanuel is also a Hebrew name, but Jesus is a Latinized Greek name. It already does not add up. Why would Mariam and Joseph name all the other sons Hebrew names but name him JESUS? The answer is they would not. Immanuel was his birth-given name, which was given by Yahweh himself.

King James named the Book of Jacob after himself and why the brother's name was changed to James. A lot of lies were put into the propagandized Christian bible to deceive mankind. They could never change Yahweh's Word, only the written Word, which they did.

Luke 2:11 For unto you is born this day in the city of David a Savior, **WHICH IS MESSIAH YAHWEH.**

John 6:42 And they said, is not this (Immanuel), the son of Joseph, whose father and mother we know? How is it then that he says, I came down from heaven?

Your scriptures may have the name Jesus, a Latinized Greek name, or Yahshua/Joshua, and not Immanuel. Let me prove to you that Immanuel was his name. Immanuel was prophesied in Isaiah 7:14 to be the name at birth. Everyone who knew him as he was growing up knew him by the name Immanuel, a Hebrew name. This was his earthly name which would have been on the tax lists and everyday living.

Isaiah 7:14 <u>Therefore Yahweh himself shall give you a sign; Behold, a</u> <u>**YOUNG WOMAN** shall conceive, and bear a son, and shall call his name</u> <u>Immanuel.</u>

Isaiah 7:14 is the prophecy for Immanuel's name. Let us compare this with when the Messenger appeared to Joseph in a dream, telling him what to name the child. You will see the contradiction. The prophecy could never have been fulfilled if the birth-given name was any other than Immanuel.

B. THOU/THEY SHALL/SHALT CALL HIS NAME IMMANUEL, JOHN, ISHMAEL, AND ISAAC.

Matthew 1:23 is the fulfillment of the Isaiah 7:14 prophecy.

Matthew 1:21 ` -- THE LIE

21 And she shall bring forth a son, and **thou shalt call his name JESUS:** for **he shall save his people from their sins.**

How the scripture should read: Matthew 1:21-23.

THE TRUTH

21. And she shall bring forth a son, and thou shalt **call his name IMMANUEL:** for he shall **save his people from their transgressions**.

22. **Now, all this was done to fulfill which was spoken of Yahweh by the prophet saying,**

23. **Behold a young woman shall be with child, and shall bring forth a son, and they shall call his name IMMANUEL, which being interpreted is Yahweh with us.**

Isaiah 7:14 is "almah" in Hebrew, and its inherent meaning is "young woman."

"Almah" Jerome translated Isa 7:14 as "virgin" in Latin: "propter hoc dabit Dominus ipse vobis signum ecce virgo concipiet et pariet filium et vocabitis nomen eius Emmanuhel" (Isa 7:14 Jerome, Latin Vulgate, 382 AD)

(Isa 7:14 Jerome, Latin Vulgate translated into English) **"Therefore, the Lord himself shall give you a sign.** Behold a virgin shall conceive **and bear a son and his name shall be called Emmanuel.**

Semiramis is Isis, who is the Virgin of virgins. Mary is just another name for Semiramis in her worship. I will try to use Mariam instead of Mary, from now on because of this. The Roman Church pushed calling Mariam the Virgin Mary because they teach she never had other children, so she was forever a virgin.

Semiramis was also known as the Holy Spirit in her pagan belief system. Osiris, the brother and husband of Semiramis/Isis, Nimrod/Osiris, just different names from different cultures for the worship of Nimrod and Semiramis, started in Babylon. Osiris/Nimrod is the "all-seeing eye" in India. It is represented by the red dot that they wear on their foreheads,

Shiva/Nimrod. Now you can see why Yahweh will destroy this Babylonian religious system that Christianity and all world religions are part of and why Christianity absorbs all these religions during the Tribulation Period to make Christianity the world religion.

Luke 1:13 But **the MESSENGER said unto him, Fear not, Zacharias:** for thy prayer is heard; and thy wife **Elisabeth shall bear thee a son**, and **THOU SHALT CALL HIS NAME JOHN.**

Genesis 16:11 And the MESSENGER of YAHWEH said unto her, Behold, thou art with child, and shalt bear a son, AND SHALT CALL HIS NAME ISHMAEL; because **YAHWEH hath heard thy affliction.**

Genesis 17:19 And Yahweh said, Sarah, thy wife shall bear thee a son indeed; AND **THOU SHALT CALL HIS NAME ISAAC: and I will establish my covenant with him for an everlasting covenant, and with his seed after him.**

NOTICE HOW THEY WERE TOLD BY THE MESSENGER TO NAME THEIR BABIES

IMMANUEL, JOHN, ISHMAEL, AND ISAAC, BUT IMMANUEL WAS CHANGED TO JESUS

AND THE REST KEPT THEIR NAMES THEY WERE TOLD TO BE CALLED. THIS WAS ALL DONE FOR DECEIT, TO DECEIVE THE WORLD WITH THE PAGAN NAME OF JESUS.

Isaiah 55:11 *So shall my word be that goeth forth out of my mouth: it shall not return unto me void,* but *it shall accomplish that which I please, and it shall prosper in the thing whereto I sent it.*

As you should be able to see in the above verses when you compare them, they put ANGEL, JESUS, SIN, LORD, AND GOD. These are all proven to be pagan sun deity names. SIN is a moon deity name. They put those into the scriptures to take the place of the true names or words, as you can see with the truth put back in those verses.

25. And knew her not till she had brought forth her firstborn son: and **he called his name IMMANUEL.**

Isaiah 8:8,10

8. And he shall pass through Judah; he shall overflow and go over, he shall reach even to the neck; and the stretching out of his wings shall fill the breadth of thy land, **O Immanuel.**

10. Take counsel together, and it shall come to naught; speak the word, and it shall not stand, for Yahweh is with us. Yahweh said his name would be Immanuel, NOT JESUS, not YAHSHUA OR ANY OTHER NAME. The name Jesus which is supposed to be a transliteration of the name Joshua or Yahshua. Let me now prove that Joshua and Jesus' names are not and never were the same name.

Jesus = English; Iesous = Greek; Iesus = Latin; No word for it in Hebrew.

The above is Jesus in English, Greek, and Latin. As you can see, there is no word in Hebrew for the name Jesus. Jesus and Joshua are not the same name.

Ask yourself, why is Jesus called Jesus in the New Testament, but Joshua is still called Joshua?

Joshua = English; You cannot translate Joshua into Greek, so they use Iesus; Josue = Latin; Yahshua = Hebrew = Yahweh salvation. The above is Joshua in English, Greek, Latin, and Hebrew. The following two verses are where they injected Jesus.

Hebrews 4:8 For if JESUS had given them rest, then would **he not afterward have spoken of another day**

Hebrews 4:8 New American Standard Version **For if JOSHUA had given them rest, <u>He would not have spoken of another day after that.</u>**

ACTS 7:45 IN THE FOLLOWING TRANSLATIONS:

Douay-Rheims Bible and the King James Bible are the only ones with the name Jesus in Acts 7:45. All the rest have Joshua, which is more proof that Jerome's Latin Vulgate was the root of the King James and why the King James has so many Latin words in it.

Douay-Rheims Bible

Which also our fathers receiving, **brought in with JESUS**, into the possession of the Gentiles, whom Yahweh drove out before the face of our fathers, unto the days of David.

King James Bible

Which also our fathers that came after **brought in with JESUS** into the possession of the Gentiles, whom God drove out before the face of our fathers, unto the days of David;

English Revised Version

Which also our fathers, in their turn, **brought in with Joshua** when they entered on the possession of the nations, which Yahweh thrust out before the face of our fathers, unto the days of David;

New International Version

After receiving the Tabernacle, our **ancestors under Joshua** brought it with them when they took the land from the nations Yahweh drove out before them. It remained in the land until the time of David,

American Standard Version

Which also our fathers, in their turn, **brought in with Joshua** when they entered on the possession of the nations, that Yahweh thrust out before the face of our fathers, unto the days of David;

And so on in the other verses below.

Berean Study Bible

And our fathers who received it <u>brought it in with Joshua</u> when they dispossessed the nations Yahweh drove out before them. It remained until the time of David.

English Revised Version

Which also our fathers, in their turn, <u>brought in with Joshua</u> when they entered on the possession of the nations, which Yahweh thrust out before the face of our fathers, unto the days of David;

World English Bible which also our fathers, in their turn, <u>brought in with Joshua</u> when they entered into the possession of the nations, whom Yahweh drove out before the face of our fathers, to the days of David.

Young's Literal Translation

Which also our fathers having in succession received, <u>did bring in with Joshua</u>, into the possession of the nations whom Yahweh did drive out from the presence of our fathers, till the days of David, **Joshua was not the given name either, just more deceit.**

CHAPTER 2

PROOF THAT THE BETHLEHEM OF GALILEE IS THE TRUE CITY OF DAVID WHERE IMMANUEL WAS BORN.

RACHEL WAS BURIED NEAR THE ROAD TO EPHRATH, WHICH IS THE BETHLEHEM OF GALILEE – NOT IN THE BETHLEHEM OF JUDAH. They left Bethel, going up to Bethlehem of Galilee, passing through Nazareth.

Genesis 35:15-20

¹⁵ And **Jacob called the name of the place where Yahweh spoke with him, Bethel.**

¹⁶ And **they journeyed from Bethel, and there was but a little way to come to Ephrath:** and Rachel travailed, and she had hard labor.

¹⁷ And it came to pass, when **she was in hard labor,** that the midwife said unto her, Fear not; thou shalt have this son also.

¹⁸ And it came to pass, **as her soul was in departing, (for she died)** that she called his name Benoni: but his father called him Benjamin.

¹⁹ **And Rachel died and was buried on the way** to **Ephrath, which is Bethlehem.**

²⁰ And **Jacob set a pillar upon her grave: that is the pillar of Rachel's grave unto this day.**

Christianity has Rachel's tomb in Bethlehem of Judah; she is not there.

CHRISTIANITY TEACHES THAT RACHEL'S TOMB IS IN THE CITY OF BETHLEHEM, JUST SOUTH OF ZION IS THE TRUE NAME.

The tomb is held in esteem by Jews, Christians, and Muslims.

DOWN ON THIS MAP (SOUTH)

The white line on the map above is the route that Rachel and Jacob took to Nazareth from Bethel, then from there taking the road to Bethlehem, the road that Rachel died on traveling to Bethlehem northwest of Nazareth, between Nazareth and Mount Carmel. Christianity wants you to believe when they left Bethel that, they headed South to Bethlehem, South of Zion, not true.

If you are traveling to the North or to the South, you would say, I'm going down South. If you were in the South going North, you would say I am going up North.

Zebulon was the last of the six sons of Jacob and Leah (Jacob's tenth son) and the founder of the Judaean Tribe of Zebulun.

The Tribe of Zebulun was one of the twelve tribes of Judaea. Following the completion of the conquest of Canaan by the Judaean tribes in the Book of Joshua, Joshua allocated the land among the twelve tribes. The territory Zebulun was allocated was at the southern end of the Galilee, with its eastern border being the Sea of Galilee, the western border being the Mediterranean Sea, the south being bordered by the Tribe of Issachar, and the north by Asher on the western side and Naphtali on the eastern.

Genesis 49:13

Zebulun shall dwell at the haven of the sea, and he *shall be* for a haven of ships, and his border *shall be* unto Zidon.

Joshua 19: 10-16

10 And the third lot came up for the children of Zebulun according to their families: and the border of their inheritance was unto Sarid:

11 And their border went up toward the sea, and Maralah, and reached to Dabbasheth, and reached to the river that is before Jokneam;

12 And turned from Sarid eastward toward the sun rising unto the border of Chislothtabor, and then goeth out to Daberath, and goeth up to Japhia,

13 And from thence passeth on along on the east to Gittahhepher, to Ittahkazin, and goeth out to Remmonmethoar to Neah;

14 And the border compasseth it on the north side to Hannathon: and the outgoings thereof are in the valley of Jiphthahel:

15 And Kattath, and Nahallal, and Shimron, and Idalah, <u>and Bethlehem:</u> <u>twelve cities with their villages.</u>

16 This is the inheritance of the children of Zebulun according to their families, these cities with their villages.

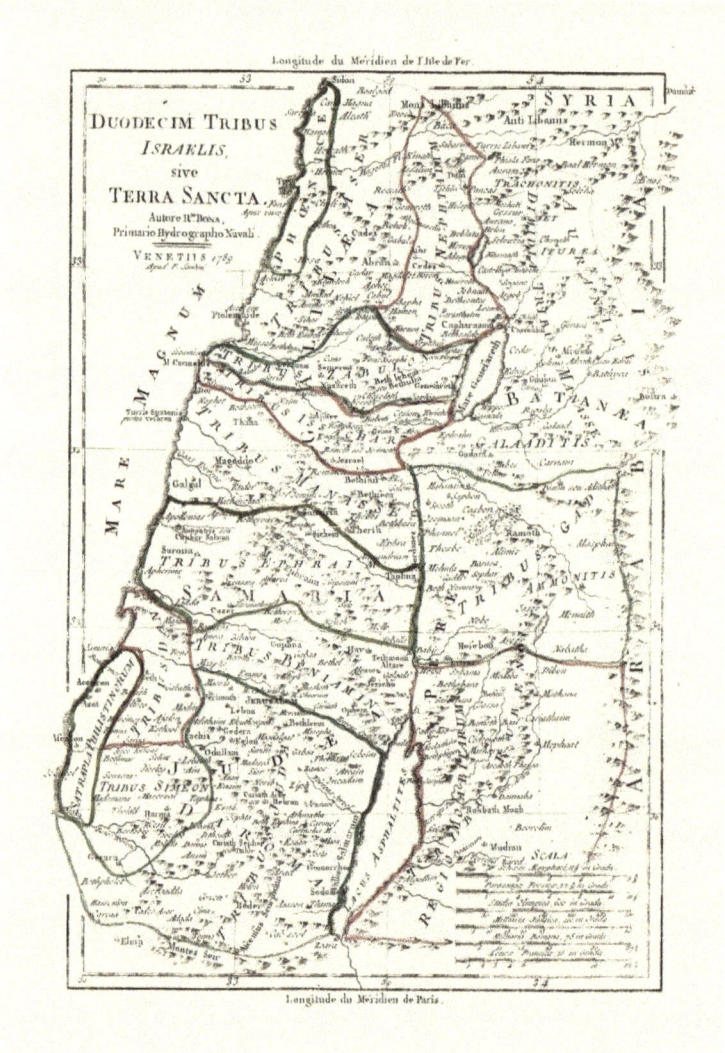

I found this old map of Judaea that shows the right divisions of the land given to each of the 12 tribes. I looked at many of them and they didn't show the true boundaries. It shows Bethlehem of Galilee, East of Nazareth, which is Northwest of Nazareth. It is hard to find a map with all the true locations if one even exists.

Bethlehem of Galilee was omitted on a lot of maps or shown in the wrong location, but I never found a map with the true boundaries of the 12 Tribes along with the true location of Bethlehem. This had to of been done on purpose to cover up the truth. That is why I must show so many different maps.

Jacob and Rachel left Bethel and went North toward Nazareth to go to Bethlehem of Galilee, around 6 miles from Nazareth. That road is where Rachel died and was buried near it.

King David's father belonged to the Ephrathite clan and lived in Bethlehem, which is why it was called <u>Ephrath, which is Bethlehem</u>. Ephrath is a description for members of the Judaean tribe of Judah, as well as for being the possible founders of Bethlehem in Galilee and why it was also called Ephrath.

CHAPTER 3

JOSEPH'S LINEAGE

1. SALMAN/SALMON

SALMON STARTED THE CITY OF BETHLEHEM, AND THOSE WHO FOLLOWED AFTER HIM IN HIS LINEUP TO IMMANUEL WERE BORN IN BETHLEHEM OF GALILEE.

1 And **these are the generations of the sons of Noah: Shem**, Ham, and Japheth, and sons were born to them after the Flood.

Genesis 10:22 The children of Shem; Elam, and Asshur, and Arphaxad, and Lud, and **Aram.**

Matthew 1:4 And Aram begat Aminadab; and Aminadab begat Naasson; and Naasson begat Salmon;

--Elimelech, Salmon (Boaz's father), the anonymous redeemer, and

Naomi's father were brothers, all the sons of Naasson, son of

Amminadab (who is explicitly mentioned at the end of the Book of Ruth as Salmon's father).

RUTH IS LOYAL TO NAOMI

Ruth 1:1-2 Before Israel/**Judaea** was ruled by kings, **Elimelech from the clan of Ephrath lived in the town of Bethlehem. His wife was named Naomi,**

THE PARADOX OF CHRISTIANITY: TRUTH THAT MAGNIFIES THE LIES

and their two sons were Mahlon and Chilion. But when their crops failed in Israel/**Judaea,** they moved to the country of Moab.[a] And while they were there, ³ Elimelech died, leaving Naomi with only her two sons.

⁴ Later, **Naomi's sons married Moabite women. One was named Orpah, and the other Ruth. About ten years later,** ⁵ **Mahlon and Chilion also died. Now Naomi had no husband or sons. ---** Nahshon/ Naasson was a son of Amminadab, **a descendant in the fifth generation of Judah.**

Salmon seems to be the one who started Bethlehem, and those following after him were born in Bethlehem of Galilee.

1 Chronicles 2:54 "The **sons of Salma/Salmon**; **Bethlehem,** and the Netophathites, Ataroth, the house of Joab, and half of the Manahethites, the Zorites."

Ruth 4:21 And Salmon begat Boaz, and Boaz begat Obed.

2. BOAZ

Ruth 4: 9-11

¹¹ And all the people that were in the gate, and the elders, said, We are witnesses. Yahweh make the woman that is come into thine house like Rachel and like Leah, which two did build the house of Judaea: and **do thou worthily in Ephratah, and be famous in Bethlehem:**

¹¹ And let thy house be like the house of Pharez, whom Tamar bare unto Judah, of the seed which Yahweh shall give thee of this young woman.

¹² **So Boaz took Ruth, and she was his wife**: and when he went in unto her, Yahweh gave her conception, and she bears a son.

15

3. OBED

He was born in Bethlehem in Galilee.

Ruth 1: 1-7

¹ Now, it came to pass in the days when the judges ruled that there was a famine in the land. And a certain **man of Bethlehem galilee** went to sojourn in the country of Moab, he, and his wife, and his two sons.

² And the name of the man was Elimelech, and the name of his wife Naomi, and the name of his two sons Mahlon and Chilion, Ephrathites of Bethlehemjudah. And they came into the country of Moab, and continued there. ³ And Elimelech Naomi's husband died; and she was left, and her two sons.

⁴ And they took them wives of the women of Moab; the name of the one was Orpah, and the name of the other Ruth: and they dwelled there about ten years.

⁵ And Mahlon and Chilion died also both of them; and the woman was left of her two sons and her husband.

⁶ Then she arose with her daughters in law, that she might return from the country of Moab: for she had heard in the country of Moab how that Yahweh had visited his people in giving them bread.

⁷ Wherefore she went forth out of the place where she was, and her two daughters in law with her; and they went on the way to return unto the land of Judah.

Naomi went back to Bethlehem in Galilee.

Ruth 4:22

And Obed begat Jesse, and Jesse begat David.

Obed was Naomi's grandson.

Ruth 4:17

And the women her neighbors gave it a name, saying, There is a son born to Naomi; and they called his name Obed: he is the father of Jesse, the father of David.

Boaz, the father of Obed, the father of Jesse, the father of King David, lived in Bethlehem of Galilee.

4. JESSE

King David's father belonged to the Ephrathite clan and lived in Bethlehem. And why it was called Ephrath, which is Bethlehem. Ephrath is a description for members of the Judaean tribe of Judah, as well as for being the possible founders of Bethlehem in Galilee and why it was also called Ephrath. (See under Salmon)

Romans 15:12 And again, Isaiah says, **"The Root of Jesse will spring up, one who will arise to rule over the nations; in him the Gentiles will hope."**

1 Samuel 17:12 Now **David was the son of that Ephrathite Ephrath of Bethlehem Galilee, whose name was Jesse;** and he had eight sons: and the man went among men for an old man in the days of Saul.

1 Samuel 16: 1,18-19

[1.] And Yahweh said unto Samuel, How long wilt thou mourn for Saul, seeing I have rejected him from reigning over Judaea? Fill thine horn with oil, and go, **I**

will send thee to Jesse the Bethlehemite: for I have provided me a king among his sons.

18 ....**T**

hen answered one of the servants, and said, Behold, **I have seen a son of Jesse the Bethlehemite,** that is cunning in playing, and a mighty valiant man, and a man of war, and prudent in matters, and a comely person, and Yahweh is with him.

19 ....**W**

herefore Saul sent messengers unto Jesse, and said, send me David thy son, which is with the sheep.

Isaiah 11:10

10 In that day the Root of Jesse will stand as a banner for the peoples; the nations will rally to him, and his resting place will be righteous.

Isaiah 11:1

1 A shoot will come up from the stump of Jesse; from his roots a Branch will bear fruit.

Bethlehem of Galilee is where Immanuel was born, not Bethlehem of Judah.

He was raised in Galilee and knew the area well.

Bethlehem means House of Bread.

John 6:35:

And Immanuel said unto them, **I am the bread of life: he that cometh to me shall never hunger, and he that believeth on me shall never thirst.**

THE BREAD OF LIFE CAME FROM THE HOUSE OF BREAD IN GALILEE.

5. KING DAVID

KING DAVID TO JOSEPH #31 IS 26 GENERATIONS THE HUSBAND OF MARIAM AND TRUE FATHER OF IMMANUEL #32.

King David was born in Bethlehem of Galilee and not Bethlehem of Judah.

1 **Samuel 17:12** Now **David was the son of that Ephrathite Ephrath of Bethlehem Galilee, whose name was Jesse;** and he had eight sons: and the man went among men for an old man in the days of Saul.

2 **Samuel 2:32** And they took up Asahel, and buried him in the sepulcher of his father, which *was in* Bethlehem. And Joab and his men went all night, and they came to Hebron at break of day.

Asahel was buried in Bethlehem of Galilee. He was a nephew of King David. He was killed in the Wilderness of Gibeon.

GIBEON IS 5 MILES NORTHWEST OF JERUSALEM/ZION AND BETHLEHEM OF JUDAH IS 5 MILES SOUTH OF ZION. IT WOULD NOT TAKE ALL NIGHT TO GO TO BETHLEHEM OF JUDAH AND BACK TO HEBRON, WHICH IS AROUND 14 MILES FROM BETHLEHEM OF JUDAH. IF IT WAS THE TRUE BETHLEHEM WHERE THEY BURIED ASAHEL.

The remains of **Gibeon** are located in the southern portion of the Palestinian village of al-Jib.

2 **Samuel 23:24 Asahel, the brother of Joab,** was one of the thirty; Elhanan, the son of Dodo of Bethlehem,

Joab with his men traveled all night to get to Hebron, a Palestinian city in the southern West Bank, 19 miles south of Zion, TO MEET BACK UP WITH DAVID.

Hebron is an **ancient biblical city in the southern West Bank, 30 kilometers (19 mi) south of Jerusalem/ZION** - BETHLEHEM OF JUDAH IS ONLY 5 MILES SOUTH OF JERUSALEM/ZION. THEY TRAVELED ALL NIGHT TO GET TO BETHLEHEM OF GALILEE TO BURY ASAH'EL IN HIS FATHER'S SEPULCHRE.

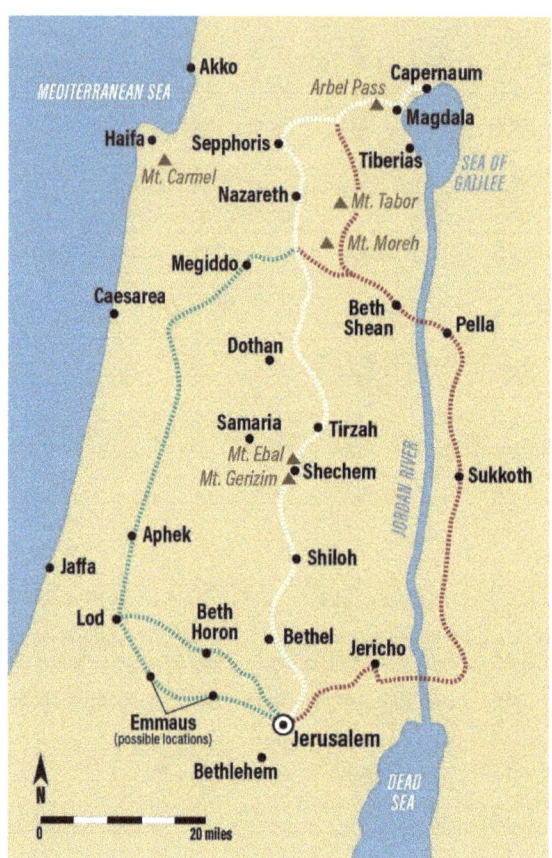

SEE ABOVE MAP: Joab buried his brother in Bethlehem in Galilee, northwest of Nazareth, the city of David, and then went to Hebron 19 miles south of Zion, and it took the army all night to get there. Hebron is not on this map but on other maps.

Zechariah 12:7 Yahweh also shall save the tents of Judah first, that the esteem of the house of David and the esteem of the inhabitants of Zion do not magnify themselves against Judah.

IMMANUEL'S LINEAGE FROM KING DAVID #5

1. **DAVID**
2. **SOLOMON**
3. **ROBOAM**
4. **ABIA**
5. **ASA**
6. **JOSEPHAT**
7. **JORAM**
8. **OZIAS**
9. **JOATHAM**
10. **ACHAZ**
11. **EZEKIAS**
12. **MANASSES**
13. **AMON**
14. **JOSIAS**
15. **JECHONIAS**
16. **SALATHIEL**
17. **ZOROBABEL**
18. **ABIUD**
19. **ELIAKIM**
20. **AZAR**
21. **SADOC**
22. **ACHIM**
23. **ELIUD**
24. **ELEAZAR**
25. **MATHAN**

26. **JACOB**

27. **JOSEPH - DESCENDED FROM THE KING LINEAGE. HUSBAND OF MARY, TRUE FATHER OF IMMANUEL.**

28. **IMMANUEL – BECAME YAHWEH MESSIAH. WILL SIT ON DAVID'S THRONE.**

KJ MICAH 5:2 "But thou, **Bethlehem Ephratah**, though **thou be little among the thousands of Judah, yet out of thee shall he come forth unto me that is to be ruler in Judaea.**

ESV Micah 5:2

2 **But you, O Bethlehem Ephrathah, who are <u>too little </u>to be among the CLANS OF JUDAEA, from you shall come forth for me one who is to be ruler in Israel, whose coming forth is <u>from of old, from ancient days.</u>**

CHAPTER 4

A. CAESAR AUGUSTUS THAT ALL THE WORLD SHOULD BE TAXED.

This chapter also proves where Immanuel was born, as the last chapter proved that Immanuel was born in Bethlehem of Galilee and not Bethlehem of Judah.

JOHN 7:42 Hath not the scripture said That **Messiah cometh of the seed of David, and out of the town of Bethlehem, where David was?**

Luke 2:1-39

¹ And it came to pass in those days that **there went out a decree from Caesar Augustus that all the world should be taxed.**

² (And this taxing was first made when Cyrenius was governor of Syria.) **QUIRINIUS IS LATIN AND IS CYRENIUS IN GREEK.**

³ And **all went to be taxed, every one into his own city. WHERE THEY WERE BORN. JOSEPH AND MARIAM WERE BOTH BORN IN BETHLEHEM OF GALILEE.**

B. 2 BETHLEHEMS

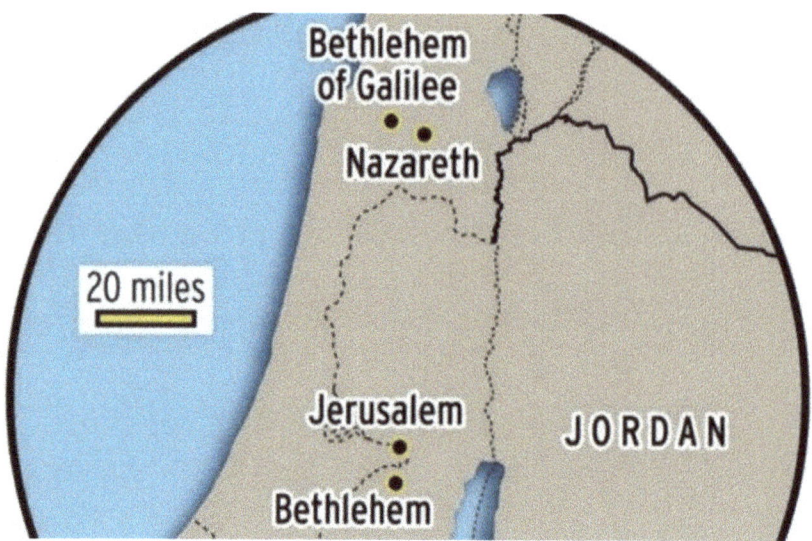

4 And Joseph also **went up out of the city of Nazareth, unto the city of David, <u>which is called Bethlehem;</u> (because he was of the house and lineage of David.)**

Joseph is shown going up to Bethlehem in Galilee, the city of David. Do you see the difference between the KJ and the NIV (below)for verse 4? It's called deceit. You cannot go up to Judah. You would have to go in a South direction.

niv4 So **Joseph also went up from the town of Nazareth in Galilee to Judea, to Bethlehem the town of David,** because he belonged to the house and line of David.

IN THIS VERSE, HE IS GOING UP OUT OF NAZARETH BUT ENDING UP GOING DOWN SOUTH TO THE BETHLEHEM IN jUDAH,5 To be taxed with Mariam, his espoused wife, **being great with child.**

Mariam could never have made that trip going south to Bethlehem riding a donkey. She was big with a child about to deliver at any time.

6 And so it was, that, **<u>while they were there, the days were accomplished that she should be delivered.</u>**

CHAPTER 5

MIGDAL EDER / TOWER OF THE SHEEP

WHAT ONE LOOKED LIKE.

Alfred Edersheim (1825 – 1889) was a Jewish convert to Christianity and a Biblical scholar known especially for his book The Life and Times of Jesus the Messiah, a book published in 1885, about "Migdal Edar" Tower of the Flock, not just any TOWER either, this was where they birthed the lambs for the House of Yahweh offerings in Zion, what a fitting place for Immanuel's birth. The title of his book is "The Life and Times of Jesus the Messiah" as the place where Immanuel was born. THIS WAS TAUGHT IN SMALL CIRCLES, SEEMS IT WAS KEPT A SECRET UNTIL LATELY A LOT MORE PEOPLE ARE TEACHING ON THAT SUBJECT BUT STILL HAS IT HAPPENING IN THE BETHLEHEM OF

JUDAEA, FROM HIS INFORMATION] that was how the shepherds knew where to go to find him since the Messenger just said, LUKE 2:12 "This shall be a sign unto you; Ye shall find the babe wrapped in swaddling clothes, lying in a manger."? What Manger? What is the truth to it? THE SHEPHERDS, who were said to be priests from the House of Yahweh, made sure the newborn lambs were without blemishes, and it is said that they would wrap the lambs in swaddling cloth to keep them from injuring themselves. WITH MORE RESEARCH TO ANSWER MY QUESTIONS, I CAME UP WITH THIS ANSWER, I READ AN ARTICLE ABOUT SHEPHERDS THAT WATCHED OVER THE SHEEP, AND THEY MADE SURE WHICH ONE WAS THE OLDEST IF THEY BIRTHED TWINS AND TO BE SURE THAT THERE WERE NO BLEMISHES OR DEFORMITIES, THEY WITNESSED THE BIRTH OF THE LAMBS. IT ALSO MENTIONED A MIGDAL EDER, MIGDAL MEANING "TOWER" AND EDER MEANING "FLOCK," A TOWER THAT WAS USED TO WATCH OVER THE FLOCK OF SHEEP. I LOOKED THE WORDS UP ON YOUTUBE TO SEE IF THERE WERE ANY VIDEOS ON IT, AND THERE ARE SOME VIDEOS TEACHINGS ON THE TOWER OF THE FLOCK. SOME ARE BETTER THAN OTHERS. THE BOTTOM ROOM WAS USED FOR A STABLE WITH STALLS TO KEEP THE SHEEP AND LAMBS SAFE DURING THE WHOLE PROCESS, SO THIS IS HOW THE SHEPHERDS KNEW WHERE TO LOOK FOR THE BABY, AND IT WOULD BE WRAPPED IN SWADDLING CLOTHES AS A SIGN TO THEM. THE SHEPHERDS WERE WITNESSES TO THE BIRTH OF THE LAMB OF YAHWEH, THAT WOULD TAKE AWAY THE TRANSGRESSIONS OF THE WORLD. THE MANGER WAS CARVED OUT OF ROCK FOR FEEDING THE SHEEP INSIDE THE BASE OF THE TOWER, A THE SHEEP STALL IS WHERE IMMANUEL LAY WHEN THEY FOUND HIM. IT WAS NOT A CAVE OR STABLE WITH VARIOUS ANIMALS LIKE CHRISTIAN MANGER SCENES SHOW.

YAHWEH DID EVERYTHING HIS WAY AND FOR HIS PURPOSE NOT BY MAN'S THINKING. CONSTANTINE TRIED COVERING UP SO MANY TRUTHS TO BRAINWASH CHRISTIANS TO ACCEPT HIS LIES; HE AND HIS MOTHER WERE

IN CAHOOTS TOGETHER. Mariam went into labor about the time they got to the Migdal Eder before entering the town of Bethlehem.

Genesis 48:7 And as for me, when I came from Padan, <u>Rachel died by me in the land of Canaan in the way, when yet there was but a little way to come unto Ephrath:</u> and <u>I buried her there in the way of Ephrath; the same is Bethlehem.</u>

Genesis 35:21 And <u>Jacob journeyed and spread his tent beyond the tower of Edar.</u> (It's Eder, but KJ has Edar.)

SAME VERSE IN THE CATHOLIC DOUAY RHEIMS

Genesis 35:21 Departing thence, <u>he pitched his tent beyond the Flock tower.</u>

<u>THIS IS THE TOWER WHERE IMMANUEL WAS BORN.</u>

A. **The manger was a carved-out rock to make a feeding trough for the sheep.**

B. **They surely put hay in the manger trough to make it more comfortable for Immanuel than having to lay on the hard rock.**

C. The base of the bottom room in the tower of the flock was used as a stall for the pregnant sheep to deliver their lambs in safety and cared for by the priest shepherds.

D. The top of the tower was used to oversee the flock of sheep.

E. The lambs were for the daily offerings at the House of Yahweh.

F. Immanuel was the final offering not just for the Hebrew people but for the whole world. **John 1:29 <u>The next day John seeth Immanuel coming unto him, and saith,</u> Behold the Lamb of Yahweh, which taketh away the transgressions of the world. How fitting under the circumstances that he was born where the offered lambs were born, only Yahweh could have made this happen.**

G. **Luke 2:22 And <u>when the days of her purification according to the law of Moses were accomplished, they brought him to Zion, to present him to Yahweh;</u>**

Micah 4:8 And thou, O tower of the flock, the stronghold of the daughter of Zion, <u>unto thee shall it come, even the first dominion; the kingdom shall come to the daughter of ZION.</u>

Micah 5:2 "But thou, Bethlehem Ephratah, though thou be little among the thousands of Judah, yet out of thee shall he come forth unto me that is to be ruler in Judea; whose goings forth have been from of old, from everlasting."

2 SAMUEL 5:7 Nevertheless <u>David took the stronghold of Zion (that *is*, the City of David).</u>

ZION WAS A FORT THAT DAVID CONQUERED; BETHLEHEM IS ALSO CALLED THE CITY OF DAVID.

King David was a shepherd.

1 SAMUEL 17:15 But <u>David went and returned from Saul to feed his</u> <u>father's sheep at Bethlehem.</u>

1 Samuel 17:34-36

[34] **And David said unto Saul, Thy servant kept his father's sheep, and there came a lion and took a lamb out of the flock: (NO BEAR)**

[35] **And I went out after him, and smote him, and delivered it out of his mouth: and when he arose against me, I caught him by his beard, and smote him, and slew him. (A LION HAS A BEARD AND NOT A BEAR, SO WHY WAS BEAR ADDED? MUST HAVE BEEN TWO DIFFERENT INSTANCES SPOKEN OF.)**

[36] **Thy servant slew both the lion and the bear: and this uncircumcised Philistine shall be as one of them, seeing he hath defied the armies of the living YAHWEH.**

I don't believe that they would have stayed in an ACTUAL inn WHERE ROOMS WERE RENTED OUT, if the town even had SUCH A PLACE. they had to stay 40 days for Mariam's purification after having a baby and Immanuel had to be circumcised "And on the eighth day, the flesh of his foreskin shall be circumcised." As you can see staying at an Inn would be expensive to do FOR THEM. THEY HAD THEIR FAMILY THERE TO HELP THEM.

Luke 2: continued

[8] And **<u>there were in the same country shepherds abiding in the field,</u> <u>keeping watch over their flock by night.</u>**

[9] And, lo, **the MESSENGER OF YAHWEH came upon them**, and **the RIGHTEOUSNESS OF YAHWEH shone round about them**: and they were sore afraid.

10 And the MESSENGER said unto them, Fear not: for, behold, I bring you good tidings of great joy, **which shall be to all people.**

11 For **unto you is born this day in the city of David a Saviour, which is MESSIAH YAHWEH.**

12 And this shall be a sign unto you; Ye shall find the babe wrapped in swaddling clothes, lying in a manger.

13 **And suddenly there was with the Messenger a multitude of the heavenly host praising YAHWEH, and saying,**

14 Praise to Yahweh in the highest heaven, and on earth peace, good will toward men.

15 And it came to pass, as the MESSENGERS were gone away from them into heaven, **the shepherds said one to another, let us now go even unto Bethlehem, and see this thing which is come to pass, which Yahweh hath made known unto us.**

16 And t**hey came with haste, and found Mariam, and Joseph, and the babe lying in a manger.**

17 **And when they had seen it, they made known abroad the saying which was told to them concerning this child.**

18 And all **they that heard it wondered at those things** which were told them by the shepherds.

19 **But Mariam kept all these things, and pondered them in her heart.**

The Shepherds happened at his birth, and they immediately went to see him.

THE WISEMEN CAME TWO YEARS AFTER HIS BIRTH.

20 **And the shepherds returned**, praising Yahweh for all the things that they had heard and seen, as it was told unto them.

²¹ And <u>when eight days were accomplished for the circumcising of the child, his name was called IMMANUEL, which was so named of the MESSENGER before he was conceived in the womb.</u>

²² And when the days of her purification according to the law of Moses were accomplished (40 days), they brought him to Zion to present him to Yahweh;

²³ (As it is written in the law of Yahweh, Every male that openeth the womb shall be called RIGHTEOUS to YAHWEH)

Luke 2:25-39

²⁵ And, behold, there was a man in Zion, whose name was Simeon; and the same man was just and devout, waiting for the consolation of Judaea: and the SPIRIT was upon him.

²⁶ And it was revealed unto him by the SPIRIT, that he should not see death, before he had seen YAHWEH'S MESSIAH.

²⁷ And he came by the Spirit into the HOUSE OF YAHWEH: and when the parents brought in the child IMMANUEL, to do for him after the custom of the law,

²⁸ Then took he him up in his arms, and blessed YAHWEH, and said,

²⁹ YAHWEH, now lettest thou thy servant depart in peace, according to thy word.

³⁰ For mine eyes have seen thy salvation,

³¹ Which thou hast prepared before the face of all people;

³² A light to lighten the Gentiles, and the Praise of thy people Judaea.

³³ And Joseph and his mother marveled at those things which were spoken of him.

34 And Simeon blessed them, and said unto Mariam his mother, Behold, this child is set for the fall and rising again of many in Judaea; and for a sign which shall be spoken against;

35 (Yea, a sword shall pierce through thy own soul also) that the thoughts of many hearts may be revealed.)

36 And there was one Anna, a prophetess, the daughter of Phanuel, of the tribe of Aser: she was of a great age, and had lived with a husband seven years from her virginity;

37 And she was a widow of about fourscore and four years, which departed not from the House of Yahweh, but served Yahweh with fastings and prayers night and day.

38 And she coming in that instant gave thanks likewise unto YAHWEH, and speak of him to all them that looked for redemption in Zion.

39 And **when they had performed all things according to the law of YAHWEH, they returned into Galilee, to their own city Nazareth.**

Joseph and Mariam were from Nazareth originally, and they went up to Bethlehem of Galilee, where Mariam, being great with child, delivered her baby Immanuel.

Matthew 2:1- 9

1 Now when Immanuel was born in Bethlehem of Galilee in the days of Herod the king, behold, there came wise men from the east to Zion.

2 Saying, Where is he that is born King of the Jews? for we have seen his star in the east, and are come to worship him.

3 When Herod the king had heard these things, he was troubled, and all Zion with him.

4 And when he had gathered all the chief priests and scribes of the people together, he demanded of them where the King should be born.

5 And they said unto him, In Bethlehem of Galilee: for thus it is written by the prophet,

Micah 5:2-4

The Messiah to Be Born in Bethlehem

2 But you, Bethlehem Ephrathah, is the smallest

town in Judah/ Galilee.

Your family is almost too small to count, but the "Ruler of

Judaea" will come from you to rule for me.

His beginnings are from ancient times, from

long, long ago.

3 Yahweh will let his people be defeated until the

woman gives birth to her child, the promised king.

6 And thou Bethlehem, in the land of Juda/Galilee, art not the least among the princes of Juda: for out of thee shall come a Governor, that shall rule my people, Israel/Judaea.

7 Then Herod, when he had privily called the wise men, enquired of them diligently what time the star appeared.

8 And he sent them to Bethlehem, and said, Go and search diligently for the young child; and when ye have found him, bring me word again, that I may come and worship him also.

9 When they had heard the king, they departed; and, lo, the star, which they saw in the east, went before them, till it came and stood over where the young child was.

CHAPTER 6

THE COMING AND VISITATION OF THE WISEMEN.

These Wisemen from Babylon were rich Jews that showed up in Zion close to 2 years after Immanuel's birth, they were not at his birth like the Christian manger scenes depict. If they were Jews from Babylon, then they would have been born there and would have registered for the census in Babylon and not in Judaea, Mary and Joseph had to go to Bethlehem of Galilee to register and while there she delivered her baby. Many Jews taken into captivity and taken to Babylon stayed in Babylon and a spacecraft showed them the way to where they were going and took them to the very house that the family was living in at Bethlehem 2 years later. Why did they go to Zion first and talked with Herod?

They would start the fulfillment of the prophecy about the killing of all the male babies 2 years old and younger with Rachel crying for her children, they did not go back to see Herod and tell him where they had found him. Yahweh in a dream told them to take another way back home and this made Herod angry and why he ordered the killings to be sure that the Messiah would also be killed.

They were also called 3 Kings, that was a later addition, there is no mention of how many there were, and all the pagan countries were the Gentile nations, there was no reason at that time for them to believe in the birth of a coming Messiah UNLESS THEY WERE Jew's. The Word of Yahweh was to the Hebrew people, not to the Gentiles at that time. He came for the lost tribes of Judaea. It was not until their disbelief that salvation was given to the Gentiles, too. Since Rome engulfed all of humanity at that time then the 10 lost tribes were still

35

within the Roman Empire boundaries. As populations moved, they also moved with them to other areas of the world. I hope you know the rest of the story.

They were Jewish Wisemen that came from Babylon in the East and were not Magi Or Kings and they showed up 2 years after Immanuel's birth when he was a toddler to bring the fulfillment of the prophecy of the male babies 2 years and younger being killed.

Matthew 2:1- 10

[1] **After IMMANUEL was born in Bethlehem in GALILEE, during the time of King Herod, Wisemen from the east came to ZION.**

[7] Then **Herod called the Wisemen secretly and found out from them the exact time the star had appeared.**

These men are called many things, Magi, Wise Men, and Kings. I believe they were Rich Jews who had come unknowingly to fulfill the prophecy of the killing of the male babies that were killed in place of Immanuel, who had learned about the birth and came to worship him. Salvation was not given to the Gentiles at that time. They were pagans or heathens and would not have come to worship the King of the Jews. I believe these Jews were part of those Jews taken in captivity to Babylon, and some Jews chose to remain in Babylon. This is why Herod killed all the male babies starting at 2 years old and younger when they did not return to Herod.

[8] **He sent them to Bethlehem** and said, "Go and search carefully for the child. As soon as you find him, report to me, so that I too may go and worship him."

HEROD HAD TO SEND THEM TO BETHLEHEM OF GALILEE; THAT IS WHERE THEY WENT; THEY THOUGHT THEY WERE FOLLOWING A STAR WHEN THEY SAW THAT IT WAS ACTUALLY A SPACECRAFT.

Bethlehem of Judah they have found nothing for the Roman Period when Immanuel walked this earth. They have found artifacts before and after that period.

Matthew 2:9-12

⁹ After they had heard the king, they went on their way, and **the star they had seen WHEN IT ROSE went ahead of them until it stopped over the place where the child was.**

Stars don't rise, but spacecraft sure do.

¹⁰ **When they saw the star, they were overjoyed.**

¹¹ And **when they were come into the house, they saw the young child with Mariam his mother, and fell down, and worshipped him**: and when they had opened their treasures, they presented unto him **gifts; gold, and frankincense and myrrh.**

FOR THE CATHOLICS, NOTICE THAT THEY DID NOT WORSHIP MARIAM.

Herod had to have sent them to Bethlehem of Galilee, not the one in Judah. These guys showed up at the house 2 years after Immanuel's birth. Christianity has them at his birth. In their manger scenes, they were not there at that time.

Bethlehem of Judah they have found nothing for the Roman Period when Immanuel walked this earth. They have found artifacts only before and after that period.

¹² And **having been warned in a dream not to go back to Herod, they returned to their country by another route.**

THEY WERE STILL LIVING IN BETHLEHEM, AND IMMANUEL WAS A TWO-YEAR-OLD CHILD LIVING IN A HOUSE.

A. JOSEPH AND MARIAM GO TO AND RETURN FROM EGYPT AND END UP LIVING IN NAZARETH AGAIN.

Matthew 2:13-15;22-23

¹³ Now *after* they had gone away, behold, a Messenger of Yahweh appeared in a dream to Joseph, saying, **"Get up, take the child and his mother and flee to Egypt,** and stay there until I tell you. For Herod is about to seek the child to destroy him."

¹⁴ So **he got up *and* took the child and his mother during the night and went away to Egypt.**

¹⁵ And **he was there until the death of Herod, in order that what was said by Yahweh through the prophet would be fulfilled, saying, Out of Egypt have I called my son**.

Matthew 2:22 But when he heard that Archelaus was reigning over Judea in place of his father Herod, he was afraid to go there, and being warned in a dream, **he took refuge in the regions of Galilee.**

Matthew 2:23 **And he came and dwelt in a city called Nazareth:** that it might be fulfilled which was spoken by the prophets, **He shall be called a Nazarene.**

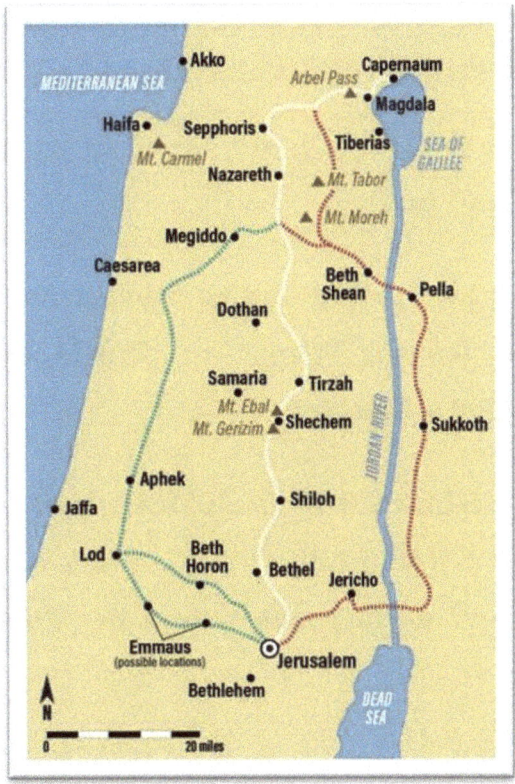

UP ON THIS MAP (NORTH DOWN ON THIS MAP (SOUTH)

This map shows pilgrimage routes from Galilee to Zion. In the first century C.E., many Jews traveled to Zion to the House of Yahweh to celebrate the Feast of Unleavened Bread, the Feast of Weeks, and the Feast of Booths.

THE WHITE LINE ON THE ABOVE MAP IS THE ROUTE THAT JACOB AND RACHEL TOOK TO NAZARETH, THEN FROM THERE, TAKING THE ROAD TO BETHLEHEM, THE ROAD RACHEL DIED ON.

A.   JOSEPH AND MARIAM RETURN TO NAZARETH

MATTHEW 2:22-23

22 But when he heard that Archelaus was reigning in Judaea in place of his father Herod, he was afraid to go there. Having been warned in a dream, **he withdrew to the district of Galilee,**

23 and he went and lived **in a town called Nazareth**. **So was fulfilled what was said through the prophets, that he would be called a Nazarene.**

Matthew 2:52 **And IMMANUEL increased in wisdom and stature, and in favor with YAHWEH and man.**

To fulfill that prophecy, they had to move from Nazareth so they could move back there after leaving Egypt, and that is why Immanuel grew up in Nazareth and was called a Nazarene.

THE BOTTOM BETHLEHEM IS IN JUDAH. LOOK AT THE MAP ON PAGE 45, TO UNDERSTAND WHAT I AM SAYING. Look what it says Bethlehem in Galilee, what they won't do to perpetuate a lie. This one is in Judah.

B. THE START OF IMMANUEL'S MINISTRY

LUKE 4:13-30

13 **And when Satan had ended all the temptation, he departed from him for a season**.

14 **And Immanuel returned in the power of the Spirit into Galilee: and there went out a fame of him through all the region round about.**

And
15 he taught in their synagogues/**cities**, being praised of all.

16 And he came to Nazareth, where he had been brought up: and, as his custom was, he went into the synagogue/**city** on the sabbath day, and stood up for to read.

17 And there was delivered unto him the book of the prophet Esaias. And when he had opened the book, he found the place where it was written,

18 The Spirit of Yahweh is upon me, because he hath anointed me to preach/ **TEACH the Word** to the poor; he hath sent me to heal the brokenhearted, to preach deliverance to the captives, and recovering of sight to the blind, to set at liberty them that are bruised,

WORD IS TRUTH; GOSPEL/SCRIPTURE IS THE LIE!

19 To preach/TEACH the acceptable year of Yahweh.

20 And he closed the book, and he gave it again to the minister, and sat down. And the eyes of all them that were in the house were fastened on him.

21 And he began to say unto them, this day is this scripture/**Word** fulfilled in your ears.

22 And all bare him witness and wondered at the gracious words which proceeded out of his mouth. And they said, Is not this Joseph's son?

23 And he said unto them, Ye will surely say unto me this proverb,

Physician, heal thyself:

whatsoever we have heard done in Capernaum, **do also here in thy country. (Meaning Galilee)**

Capernaum was in Judaea in the Northern part of the Sea of Galilee. He did a lot of teaching around the Sea of Galilee area. Capernaum was a town of Jews until the Assyrians took a lot of them and replaced them with Gentiles, and how it ended up being a Samaritan town. Jews breeding with Gentiles.

Matthew 4:15-17

15 "The **land of Zebulun and the land of Naphtali,** *By* **the way of the sea, beyond the Jordan**, **Galilee of the Gentiles:**

16 The **people who sat in darkness have seen a great light**,

And **upon those who sat in the region and shadow of death Light has dawned.**"

17 **From that time Immanuel began to teach and to say, "Repent, for the kingdom of Yahweh is at hand."**

24 And he said, Verily I say unto you, **No prophet is accepted in his own country.**

25 But I tell you of a truth, many widows were in Judaea in the days of Elijah, when the heaven was shut up three years and six months, when great famine was throughout all the land;

26 But unto none of them was Elijah sent, save unto Sarepta, a city of Sidon, unto a woman that was a widow.

27 And many lepers were in Judea in the time of Eliseus/Elisha the prophet; and none of them was cleansed, saving Naaman the Syrian.

28 And all they in the synagogue/**city**, when they heard these things, were filled with wrath,

29 And rose up, and thrust him out of the city, and led him unto the brow of the hill whereon their city was built, that they might cast him down headlong.

And

30 But he passing through the midst of them went his way,

Luke 4:14-24

14 Immanuel returned in the power of the Spirit into Galilee: and there and there **went out a fame of him through all the region round about.** **15** And he taught in their synagogues/**cities**, being esteemed of all.

16 And he came to Nazareth, where he had been brought up: and, as his custom was, he went into the synagogue/**city** on the sabbath day and stood up for to read.

17 And **there was delivered unto him the book of the prophet Esaias/ISAIAH**. And when he had opened the book, he found the place where it was written,

18 The Spirit of Yahweh is upon me, because he hath anointed me to teach the Word to the poor; he hath sent me to heal the brokenhearted, to teach deliverance to the captives, and recovering of sight to the blind, to set at liberty them that are bruised,

19 To teach the acceptable year of Yahweh.

20 And he closed the book, and he gave it again to the minister/**RABBI/TEACHER,** and sat down. And the eyes of all of them that were in the synagogue/**city** were fastened on him.

21 And he began to say unto them, **this day is this scripture fulfilled in your ears.**

22 And all bare him witness and wondered at the gracious words which proceeded out of his mouth. And they said, Is not this Joseph's son?

23 And he said unto them, Ye will surely say unto me this proverb, Physician, heal thyself: whatsoever **we have heard done in Capernaum, do also here in thy country.**

24 And he said, Verily I say unto you, **no prophet is accepted in his own country.**

Jews did not use synagogues; moon worshipers did. Sin-A-God two moon deity names to make that word. Sun worshipers used Temples.

Luke 2:40-52

40 And **the child grew, and waxed strong in spirit, filled with wisdom: and the SPIRIT of YAHWEH was upon him.**

41 Now his parents went to Jerusalem/ **[Bethlehem] every year** at the **feast of the Passover.**

42 And when he was twelve years old, **they went UP to Jerusalem/[Bethlehem]** after the custom of the feast.

YOU CANNOT GO UP TO JERUSALEM/ZION. THEY WERE IN NAZARETH. THE BETHLEHEM BEING SPOKEN OF IS THE ONE IN GALILEE. SEE HOW THEY PUSH THE BETHLEHEM OF JUDAH LIE.

43 And when they had fulfilled the days, as they returned, the child IMMANUEL tarried behind in BETHLEHEM; and Joseph and his mother knew not of it.

44 But they, supposing him to have been in the company, went a day's journey; and they sought him among their kinsfolk and acquaintance.

45 And when they found him not, they turned back again to BETHLEHEM, seeking him.

46 And it came to pass, that after three days they found him in the temple/**CITY,** sitting in the midst of the doctors, both hearing them, and asking them questions.

47 And all that heard him were astonished at his understanding and answers.

And

⁴⁸ when they saw him, they were amazed: and his mother said unto him, Son, why hast thou thus dealt with us? Behold, thy father and I have sought thee sorrowing.

⁴⁹ And he said unto them, how is it that ye sought me? Wist ye not that I must be about my Father's business?

⁵⁰ And they understood not the saying which he spake unto them.

⁵¹ And **he went UP with them, and came to Nazareth,** and was subject unto them: but his mother kept all these sayings in her heart. **THE LIE.**

Luke 2:51 And he went DOWN with them, and came to Nazareth, and was subject unto them: but his mother kept all these sayings in her heart. **THE TRUTH**

CHAPTER 7

PROVE ALL THINGS!

1 THESSALONIANS 5:21

Prove all things; hold fast that which is good.

MARK 5:35,36,38

³⁵ While he yet spake, there came from the ruler of the synagogue's/city *house certain* which said, thy daughter is dead: why troublest thou the Master any further?

³⁶ As soon as Immanuel heard the word that was spoken, he saith unto the ruler of the synagogue/city, Be not afraid, only believe.

38 And he cometh to the house of the ruler of the synagogue/city, and seeth the tumult, and them that wept and wailed greatly.

There are 50 verses or more with synagogue in them or synagogues that replaced the words city and cities and are proven when you read the verses.

Acts 6:9 Then there arose certain of the **synagogue/city**, which is called the **synagogue/city** of the Libertines, and Cyrenians, and Alexandrians, and of them of Cilicia and of Asia, disputing with Stephen.

John 6:59 These things said he in the **synagogue/city**, as he taught in Capernaum.

Luke 7:5 For he loveth our nation, and he hath built us a **synagogue/city**.

Matthew 12:9 And when he was departed thence, he went into their **synagogue/city**:

Mark 1:23 And there was in their **synagogue/city** a man with an unclean spirit; and he cried out,

Luke 4:28 And all they in the **synagogue/city** when they heard these things, were filled with wrath,

Acts 17:1 Now when they had passed through Amphipolis and Apollonia, they came to Thessalonica, where was a **synagogue/city** of the Jews:

Luke 4:33 And in the **synagogue/city** there was a man, which had a spirit of an unclean devil, and cried out with a loud voice,

Mark 5:36 As soon as Jesus heard the word that was spoken, he saith unto the ruler of the **synagogue/city**, be not afraid, only believe.

Mark 3:1 And he entered again into the **synagogue/city**; and there was a man there which had a withered hand.

Acts 22:19 And I said, Master, they know that I imprisoned and beat in every **synagogue/city** them that believed on thee:

Mark 1:21 And they went into Capernaum; and straightway on the sabbath day he entered into the synagogue/city and taught.

CHAPTER 8

THE ROOT IS YAHWEH MESSIAH, THE BROKEN-OFF BRANCHES ARE JEWS, AND THE GRAFTED-IN BRANCHES ARE THE GENTILES.

Romans 11:16-24

16 For if the first Fruit (MESSIAH YAHWEH) be righteous, the lump is also righteous: and if the root be righteous, so are the branches.

17 And if some of the branches be broken off, and thou, being a wild olive tree, were grafted in among them, and with them partakest of the root and fatness of the olive tree;

18 Boast not against the branches. But if thou boast, thou bearest not the root, but the root thee.

19 Thou wilt say then, the branches were broken off, that I might be grafted in.

20 Well; because of unbelief they were broken off, and thou standest by faith. Be not high-minded, but fear:

21 For if YAHWEH spared not the natural branches, take heed lest he also spare not thee.

²¹ Behold therefore the goodness and severity of YAHWEH: on them which fell, severity; but toward thee, goodness, if thou continue in his goodness: otherwise, thou also shalt be cut off.

²² <u>And they also, if they abide not still in unbelief, shall be grafted in: for YAHWEH is able to graft them in again.</u>

²³ <u>For if thou wert cut out of the olive tree which is wild by nature, and wert grafted contrary to nature into a good olive tree: how much more shall these, which be the natural branches, be grafted into their own olive tree?</u>

LAW AND FAITH

Ephesians 3:6-7

⁶ That the Gentiles should be fellow heirs, and of the same body, and partakers of his promise in Yahweh by the WORD:

⁷ Whereof I was made a minister, according to the gift of the SPIRIT of YAHWEH given unto me by the effectual working of his power.

Galatians 3:

O foolish Galatians, who hath bewitched you, that ye should not obey the truth, before whose eyes YAHWEH MESSIAH hath been evidently set forth, KILLED among you?

---

¹ This only would I learn of you, Received ye the Spirit by the works of the law, or by the hearing of faith?

² Are ye so foolish? Having begun in the Spirit, are ye now made perfect by the flesh?

³ Have ye suffered so many things in vain? If it be yet in vain.

⁵ He therefore that ministereth to you the Spirit, and worketh miracles among you, doeth he it by the works of the law, or by the hearing of faith?

⁶ Even as Abraham believed Yahweh, and it was accounted to him for righteousness.

⁷ Know ye therefore that they which are of faith, the same are the children of Abraham.

⁸ And the scripture, foreseeing that YAHWEH would justify the heathen through faith, taught before the WORD unto Abraham, saying, in thee shall all nations be blessed.

⁹ So then they which be of faith are blessed with faithful Abraham.

¹⁰ For as many as are of the works of the law are under the curse: for it is written, Cursed is every one that continueth not in all things which are written in the book of the law to do them.

¹¹ But that no man is justified by the law in the sight of YAHWEH, it is evident: for the just shall live by faith.

¹² And the law is not of faith: but the man that doeth them shall live in them.

¹³ YAHWEH hath redeemed us from the curse of the law, being made a curse for us: for it is written, Cursed is every one that hangeth on a tree:

¹⁴ That the blessing of Abraham might come on the Gentiles through YAHWEH MESSIAH; that we might receive the promise of the Spirit through faith.

¹⁵ Brethren, I speak after the manner of men; Though *it be* but a man's covenant, yet *if it be* confirmed, no man disannulleth, or addeth thereto.

¹⁶ Now to Abraham and his seed were the promises made. He saith not, And to seeds, as of many; but as of one, And to thy seed, which is Yahweh.

¹⁷ And this I say, *that* the covenant, that was confirmed before of Yahweh in Messiah, the law, which was four hundred and thirty years after, cannot disannul, that it should make the promise of none effect.

¹⁸ For if the inheritance *be* of the law, *it is* no more of promise: but Yahweh gave *it* to Abraham by promise.

¹⁹ Wherefore then *serveth* the law? It was added because of transgressions, till the seed should come to whom the promise was made; *and it was* ordained by Messengers in the hand of a mediator.

²⁰ Now a mediator is not *a mediator* of one, but Yahweh is one.

²¹ Is the law then against the promises of Yahweh? Yahweh forbid: for if there had been a law given which could have given life, verily righteousness should have been by the law.

²² But the scripture hath concluded all under transgression, that the promise by faith of Yahweh Messiah might be given to them that believe.

²³ But before faith came, we were kept under the law, shut up unto the faith which should afterward be revealed.

²⁴ Wherefore the law was our schoolmaster *to bring us* unto Yahweh, that we might be justified by faith.

²⁵ But after that faith is come, we are no longer under a schoolmaster.

²⁶ For ye are all the children of Yahweh by faith in Yahweh Messiah.

²⁷ For as many of you as have been baptized into Yahweh have put on Yahweh is neither Jew nor Greek, there is neither bond nor free, there is neither male nor female: for ye are all one in Messiah Yahweh.

BAPTIZED IN THE SPIRIT OF YAHWEH, THAT IS WHAT MAKES A JEW OR GENTILE ONE A JUDAEAN.

29 <u>And if ye be Yahweh's, then are ye Abraham's seed, and heirs according to the promise.</u>

Colossians 3:11 <u>Where there is neither Greek nor Jew, circumcision nor uncircumcision, Barbarian, Scythian, bond *nor* free: but Yahweh *is* all, and in all.</u>

Philippians 3:3 <u>For we are the circumcision, which worship Yahweh in the Spirit, and rejoice in Messiah Yahweh, and have no confidence in the flesh.</u>

The above is the true teaching, today you will notice that Christians and people who are in these Messianic and Judaism movements, which are nothing but warmed over Christianity and are trying to be correct today, will see them use Jesus, Yahshua, Yeshua, Yehoshua, thinking Judaism is correct, but it's not, even to the fact they try showing Christianity as true.

Why is there no House of Yahweh? The Messiah became the last and final offered Lamb for transgressions, and he did away with what we call Judaism, so no more collecting tithes, which only the Levite priests could do those things, so the Levites were no longer needed and why the House of Yahweh was destroyed in 70 C.E. Yahweh put His Spirit into the believers back then, whose bodies became the House of Yahweh for the people back then to the coming 7 Year Peace Plan elect. So, there is no reason for the House of Yahweh built with hands.

Yahweh Messiah builds the third House of Yahweh during his Millennial Kingdom and reinstitutes the Levi priests at that time.

Salvation comes again during the 7-Year Peace Plan that ends WW3. Those who have died from Constantine's reign, who had killed the last of Yahweh's elect with his 11th Emperor persecution that never heard the truth up to those who die right before the period of salvation being given again during the 7 Year Peace Plan, Yahweh will raise them up during the Millennial Kingdom and teach them Himself. The reason for the reinstitution of the Levites.

There will be no excuses for not knowing the whole truth. So, each person will end up choosing who they will serve, Satan and eternal death, where a person will never exist again, or Yahweh and eternal life.

CHAPTER 9

TEN COMMANDMENT DECEPTION:

Are the Ten Commandments Done Away With?

The 10 Commandments were never done away with, but this is Satan's world, and there is no salvation. Not only that but people cannot keep the 10 Commandments without Yahweh's Spirit infilling. The Hebrew people had the Levite priesthood to offer offerings for their transgressions, which were done away with when Yahweh did away with the House of Yahweh worship along with animal offerings, the Levite priesthood, and what is known as Judaism.

There are three (3) sets of the 10 Commandments that Christianity uses. One is what most protestant denominations use; the Jehovah's Witnesses have a different one also, and then there's the one the Catholic denomination uses:

PROTESTANT TEN COMMANDMENTS:

1. Thou shalt have no other **gods** before me.
2. Thou shalt not make unto thee any graven image.
3. Thou shalt not take the name of the **Lord** thy **God** in vain.
4. Remember the Sabbath day and keep it **holy**.
5. Honor thy father and thy mother.

6. Thou shalt not **kill**.

7. Thou shalt not commit adultery.

8. Thou shalt not steal.

9. Thou shalt not bear false witness against thy neighbor.

10 Thou shalt not covet.

Notice that they use "God and Lord" (which are pagan deity names) in theirs. They took Yahweh's name out. They have "kill" instead of murder in the 6th commandment. "Holy" has to do with the sun.

The American Heritage Dictionary (based on the New Second College Edition), copyright 1983:

MURDER = Taking innocent blood.

JEHOVAH WITNESS TEN COMMANDMENTS:

1.	I am **Jehovah** your **God**, who brought you out of the land of Egypt, out of the house of slaves. You must never have any other **gods** against my face.
2.	You must not make for yourself a carved image, any form like anything that is in the heavens above or that is on the earth underneath, or that is in the waters under the earth. You must not bow down to them or be led to serve them because I, **Jehovah** your **God,** am a **God** exacting exclusive devotions, bringing punishment for the error of fathers upon sons and upon the third generation and upon the fourth generation, in the case of those who hate me; but exercising loving-kindness toward the thousandth generation in

the case of those who love me and keep my commandments.

3.   You must not take up the Name of **Jehovah** your **God** in a worthless way, for **Jehovah** will not leave anyone unpunished who takes up his name in a worthless way.

4.   Keeping the Sabbath day to hold sacred, just as **Jehovah** your **God** commanded you, you are to render service, and you must do all your work for six days. But the seventh day is a Sabbath to **Jehovah** your **God**. You must not do any work, you nor your son nor your daughter nor your slave man nor your slave girl nor your bull nor your ass nor any domestic animal inside your gates, in order that your slave man and your slave girl may rest the same as you.

5.   Honor your father and your mother, just as Jehovah your **God** has commanded you, in order that your days may prove long and it may go well with you on the ground that **Jehovah** your **God** is giving you.

6.   You must not murder.

7.   Neither must you commit adultery.

8.   Neither must you steal.

9.   Neither must you testify to a falsehood against your fellowman.

10.   Neither must you desire your fellowman's wife. Neither must you selfishly crave your fellowman's house, his field, his slave man, or his slave girl. His bull or his **ass** or anything that belongs to your fellow man.

Jehovah's Witnesses use Jehovah and God, which the word Jehovah did not exist until the latter 15 or 16 century, which is a Latin word that came from Germany and a German priest. It was used exclusively during the Roman Empire after its creation. That's how it got into the King James Scriptures. Notice they do not use the word "holy." Notice they use the word murder and not "kill." <u>CATHOLIC TEN COMMANDMENTS:</u>

1.	I am the **Lord** thy **God**; thou shalt not have strange **Gods** before me.
2.	Thou shalt not take the name of the **Lord** thy **God** in vain.
3.	Remember thou, keep **holy** the **Lord's** day.
4.	Honor thy Father and thy Mother.
5.	Thou shalt not **kill**.
6.	Thou shalt not commit adultery.
7.	Thou shalt not steal.
8.	Thou shalt not bear false witness against thy neighbor.
9.	Thou shalt not covet thy neighbor's wife.
10	Thou shalt not covet thy neighbor's goods.

Notice the Catholics also use "God and Lord" and not Yahweh's name in them. Notice that the

Catholics are the same as the Protestants, except that they took out the 2nd commandment completely and made the 3rd commandment the 2nd. They split the 10th commandment to make it the 9th and 10th to make up for taking out the 2nd one, which is: (Thou shalt not make thee any graven image or any likeness of anything that is in heaven above or that is in the earth beneath or that is in the waters beneath the earth; Thou shalt not bow down thyself unto them nor serve them.) Also, they use "kill" instead of murder here too. They use Lord's Day, and Lord is a sun deity name. The meaning of Lord's Day is Sunday, the day pagans worshiped the sun under many different names.

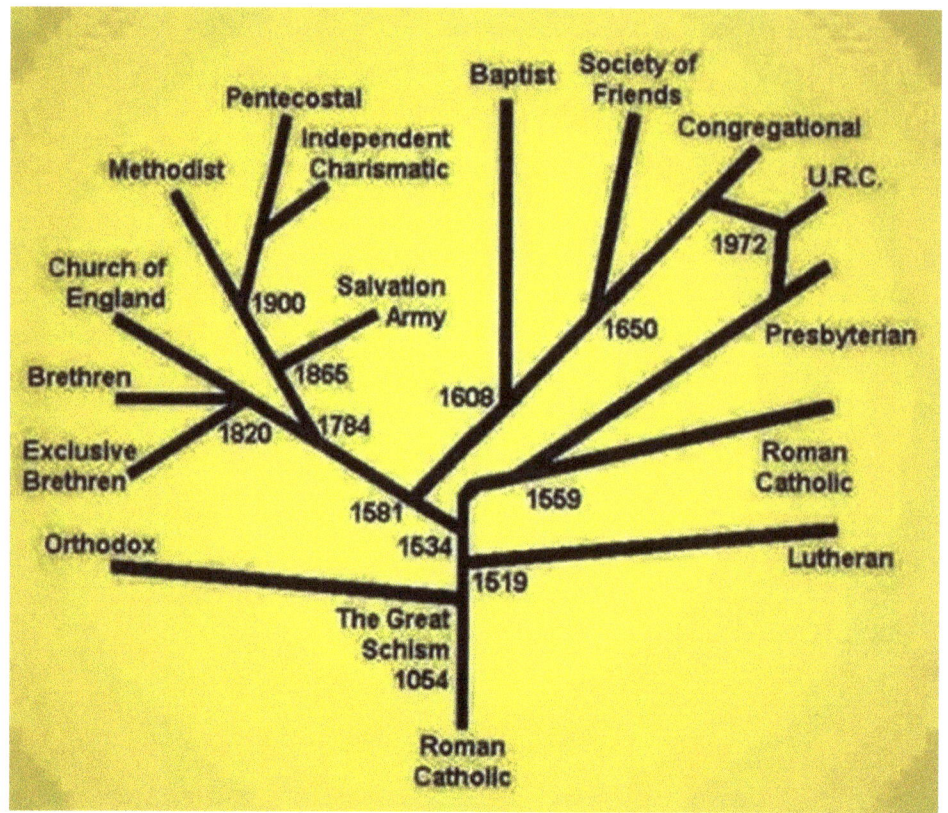

Whoever made this chart is perfectly accurate. It starts with Roman Catholic, that would stand for the Roman Universal/ Catholic religion of Christianity that was started by Constantine in 312 C.E. Then, in 1559, it has Roman Catholic again, but this time, it is the denomination started in 1559 at the Council of Trent to counter the Reformation. You can see how Christianity branched off into denominations and why the Pope is over all Christianity, no matter what denomination it is.

YAHWEH'S TEN COMMANDMENTS:

1	I am Yahweh, who has brought you out of Egypt, out of the house of bondage. You shall have no other deities before Me.

2   You shall not make yourself a graven image, or any likeness of anything that is in heaven above, or that is in the earth beneath, or that is in the water under the earth; you shall not bow down to them or serve them; for I Yahweh am a jealous Mighty One, visiting the iniquity of the fathers upon the children to the third and the fourth generation of those who hate Me, but showing mercy to thousands of them that love Me and keep My commandments.

3   You shall not make wrong use of the Name of Yahweh; Yahweh will not leave unpunished the man who misuses His Name.

4   Remember the Sabbath day to keep it set apart. Six days shall you labor, and do all your work: but the seventh day is a Sabbath of Yahweh your Almighty; in it you shall not do any work, you, or your son, or your daughter, your manservant, or your maidservant, or your cattle, or the stranger that is within your gates; for in six days Yahweh made heaven and earth, the sea, and all that is in them, and rested the seventh day; therefore, Yahweh blessed the Sabbath day and set it apart.

5   Honor your father and your mother, that your days may be long in the land that Yahweh gives you.

6   You shall not commit murder.

7	You shall not commit adultery.
8	You shall not steal.
9	You shall not bear false witness against your neighbor.
10	You shall not covet your neighbor's house, you shall not covet your neighbor's wife, or his manservant, or his maidservant, or his ox, or his donkey, or anything that is your neighbor's.

Notice the word ass has been replaced by donkey. Not only is there a pagan deity by the name of

"Ass" of the Asgard, but also humanity has made it a cuss word. So, to purify that part of the commandment, it has been replaced with the proper word "donkey."

As you can see all three 10 commandments above are not true and very deceptive. Using "Lord and God," which are pagan sun deity names and using the word "holy" derived from the divinely honored sun. Not giving Yahweh His due worship and honor.

As you can see, the different 10 Commandments used within Christianity cause mass confusion, which is what Mystery Babylon is.

Jacob 2:10 For whosoever shall keep the whole law, and yet offend in one point, he is guilty of all.

Galatians 5:18 But if ye be led of the Spirit, ye are not under the law.

No one can keep the Commandments without Yahweh's Spirit infilling that gives salvation to a person.

1 John 3:24 And he that keepeth His commandments dwelleth in Him, and He in him. And hereby we know that He abideth in us, by the Spirit which He hath given us.

Ezekiel 36:27 And I will put My Spirit within you and cause you to walk in my statutes, and ye shall keep my judgments and do them.

Romans 8:9 But ye are not in the flesh, but in the Spirit, if so be that the Spirit of Yahweh dwell in you. Now if any <u>have not the Spirit of Yahweh, he is none of His.</u>

2 Corinthians 13:5 Examine yourselves to see whether you are in the faith; test yourselves. Do you not realize that Messiah Yahweh is in you unless, of course, you fail the test?

Is Matthew 22:37 & 39 two (2) new commandments to do away with the Ten Commandments? The answer is NO.

Matthew 22:37-38

37   **Immanuel** said unto him, Thou shalt love Yahweh with all thy heart, and with all thy soul, and with all thy mind.

38   This is the first and great commandment.

Notice that this covers the first four (4) commandments to do unto Yahweh.

1. **I am Yahweh, who has brought you out of Egypt, out of the house of bondage. You shall have no other deities before Me.**

2. **You shall not make yourself a graven image, or any likeness of anything that is in heaven above, or that is in the earth beneath, or that is in the water under the earth; you shall not bow down to them or serve them; for I Yahweh your Almighty, I am a jealous one, visiting the iniquity of the fathers upon the children to the third and the fourth generation of those who hate Me, but showing mercy to thousands of them that love Me and keep My commandments.**

3. **You shall not make wrong use of the Name of Yahweh; Yahweh will not leave unpunished the man who misuses His Name.**

4. **Remember the Sabbath day, to keep it separate. Six days shall you labor, and do all your work: but the seventh day is a Sabbath of Yahweh; in it you shall not do any work, you, or your son, or your daughter, your manservant, or your maidservant, or your cattle, or the stranger that is within your gates; for in six days Yahweh made heaven and earth, the sea, and all that is in them, and rested the seventh day; therefore, Yahweh blessed the Sabbath day and set it apart.**

Matthew 22:39 39: And the second is like unto it, thou shalt love thy neighbor as thyself.

☛ *Notice that this covers the last six (6) commandments to do with your fellow man.*

5. Honor your father and your mother, that your days may be long in the land that Yahweh your Almighty gives you.

6. You shall not commit murder.

7. You shall not commit adultery.

8. You shall not steal.

9. You shall not bear false witness against your neighbor.

10. You shall not covet your neighbor's house, you shall not covet your neighbor's wife, or his manservant, or his maidservant, or his ox, or his donkey, or anything that is your neighbor's.

CHAPTER 10

A. ARE THERE CONTRADICTIONS WITH THE JUDAS STORY?

How did Judas Iscariot die according to how Matthew 27:5 puts it or how Paul puts it in Acts 1:18?

Matthew 27:5

5 And he cast down the pieces of silver in the House, and departed, and went and hanged himself.

Acts 1:18

18 Now this man purchased a field with the reward of iniquity; and falling headlong, he burst asunder in the midst, and all his bowels gushed out.

BOTH ARE TRUE. HE HUNG HIMSELF, HIS BODY ROTTED, and falling headlong, he burst asunder in the midst, and all his bowels gushed out." SO NO ONE TOOK HIM DOWN, AND HE ROTTED WHILE HANGING, then THE ROPE ROTTED AND BROKE.

Judas threw the money in one verse, and in the other, he used it to purchase a field where he died?

Matthew 27:3-5

3. When Judas, who had betrayed him, saw that Immanuel was condemned, he was seized with remorse and returned the thirty pieces of silver to the chief priests and the elders.

4. "I have transgressed," he said, "for I have betrayed innocent blood." "What is that to us?" they replied. "That's your responsibility."

5. So Judas threw the money into the House [of Yahweh] and left. Then he went away and hanged himself. JUDAS STILL HAD THE 30 PIECES OF SILVER AND THREW THEM ALL BACK AT THEM. Returned the thirty pieces of silver to the chief priests and the elders. So he did not buy the land himself, SO WHO DID?

MATTHEW 27:6-10

6. And the chief priests took the silver pieces, and said, It is not lawful for to put them into the treasury, because it is the price of blood.

7. And they took counsel, and bought with them the potter's field, to bury strangers in.

8. Wherefore that field was called, The field of blood, unto this day.

9. Then was fulfilled that which was spoken by Jeremiah the prophet, saying, And they took the thirty pieces of silver, the price of him that was valued, whom they of the children of Judea did value;

10. And gave them for the potter's field, as YAHWEH appointed me. The CHIEF PRIESTS BOUGHT THE FIELD.

B. DO THIS IN REMEMBRANCE OF ME:

John 6:51

"**I am the living bread that came down from heaven.** If anyone eats of this bread, he will live forever. And **the bread that I will give for the life of the world is my flesh.**"

Isaiah 53:5

But **he was wounded for our transgressions;** he was crushed for our iniquities; **upon him was the chastisement that brought us peace**, and **with his stripes we are healed.**

IMMANUEL TOLD THE ELECT BACK THEN TO DO ONE THING IN REMEMBRANCE OF HIM, DONE ONCE A YEAR, ON PASSOVER;

He created a new way for the New Covenant. With him as the perfect offering, He ended the Old Covenant and established the New Covenant.

Luke 22:13-20

¹³ And they went and found as he had said unto them: and they made ready the Passover.

¹⁴ And when the hour had come, he sat down, and the twelve apostles with him.

¹⁵ And he said unto them, with desire I have desired to eat this Passover with you before I suffer:

¹⁶ For I say unto you, I will not any more eat thereof, until it be fulfilled in the kingdom of Yahweh.

17 And he took the cup, and gave thanks, and said, take this, and divide it among yourselves:

18 For I say unto you, <u>I will not drink of the fruit of the vine, until the kingdom of Yahweh shall come.</u>

19 <u>And he took bread, and gave thanks, and break it, and gave unto them, saying, this is my body which is given for you: this do in remembrance of me.</u>

20 Likewise also the cup after supper, saying, <u>this cup is the New Covenant in my blood</u>, which is shed for you.

1 Corinthians 10:17

<u>Because there is one bread, we who are many are one body, for we all partake of the one bread.</u>

1 Corinthians 11:23-28, 30,32

23 For <u>I received from Yahweh what I also delivered to you,</u> **that Yahweh on the night when he was betrayed took bread.**

24 <u>And when he had given thanks, he broke it, and said,</u> **"This is my body which is for you. Do this in remembrance of me."**

25 <u>In the same way also he took the cup,</u> **after supper**, saying, <u>**"This cup is the new covenant in my blood. Do this**, as often as you drink it, in remembrance of me."</u>

26..

....F or as often as you eat this bread and drink the cup, you proclaim Yahweh's death until he comes.

27..

....Whoever, therefore, eats the bread or drinks the cup of Yahweh in an unworthy manner will be guilty concerning the body and blood of Yahweh.

<u>28 Let a person examine himself, then, and so eat of the bread and drink of the cup.</u>

30 That is **<u>why many of you are weak and ill, and some have died.</u>**

32 But **<u>when we are judged by Yahweh, we are disciplined so that we may not be condemned along with the world.</u>**

<u>The bread and cup are only symbolic of what he had done. Those back then kept the Passover in a new way and were not actually eating his body and drinking his blood. That is against what the scriptures teach and would be cannibalism. They had to drain all the blood from the offered lamb and any other animal that was offered.</u>

<u>The Spirit-filled Elect back then could not take it unworthily. Only those that were lost could.</u>

1 Corinthians 5:7

Cleanse out the old leaven that you may be a new lump, as you really are unleavened. **<u>For Yahweh, our Passover lamb, has been offered.</u>**

1 John 1:3

That which we have seen and heard we proclaim also to you, so that you too may have fellowship with us; and **<u>indeed, our fellowship is with the Father and with his Son Yahweh Messiah.</u>**

1 John 1:7

But if we walk in the light, as he is in the light, we have fellowship with one another, and **<u>the blood of Yahweh his Son cleanses us from all transgression.</u>**

C. "FEAR NOT" OR "DO NOT BE AFRAID."

The phrase "Fear not." or "Do not be afraid" appears many times in the scriptures. When Yahweh pours out the Latter Rain of His Spirit on those who believe, then and only then will people understand that phrase during the Tribulation Period. The following are a few verses that go along with that Period and to Fear Not.

Isaiah 35:4 - "Say to them that are of a fearful heart, be strong, fear not: behold, your Yahweh will come with vengeance, even Yahweh with a recompence; he will come and save you."

Psalm 23:4 - "Yea, though I walk through the valley of the shadow of death, **I will fear no evil: for thou art with me; thy rod and thy staff they comfort me.**"

Matthew 10:28 "And **do not fear those who kill the body but cannot kill the soul.** But **rather fear Him who is able to destroy both soul and body in the Lake of Fire.**"

Revelation 2:10 "**Do not fear any of those things which you are about to suffer. Indeed, the devil is about to throw some of you into prison, that you may be tested, and you will have tribulation ten days. Be faithful until death, and I will give you the crown of life.**"

D. YAHWEH'S SEAL

John 3:33,3

33. He that hath received his testimony hath **set to his seal** that Yahweh is true.

34. For he whom Yahweh hath sent speaketh the words of Yahweh: for **Yahweh giveth not the Spirit by measure unto him**.

John 6:27 Labor not for the meat which perisheth, but for that meat which endureth unto everlasting life, which the Son of man shall give unto you: for **him hath Yahweh the Father Sealed**

Revelation 7:2-4

2. And I saw another Messenger ascending from the east, **having the seal of the living Yahweh**: and he cried with a loud voice to the four Messengers, to whom it was given to hurt the earth and the sea.

3. Saying, hurt not the earth, neither the sea, nor the trees, **till we have sealed** the servants of Yahweh in their forehead.

4. And I heard the number **of them which were sealed**: and **there were sealed** a hundred and forty and four thousands of all the tribes of the children of Israel.

Revelation 5:1-6

1. And I saw in the right hand of him that sat on the throne a book written within and on the backside, **sealed with seven seals.**

2. And I saw a strong Messenger proclaiming with a loud voice, who is worthy to open the book, and to lose the seals thereof?

3. And no man in heaven, nor in earth, neither under the earth, was able to open the book, neither to look thereon.

4. And I wept much, because no man was found worthy to open and to read the book, neither to look thereon.

5. And one of the elders saith unto me, Weep not: behold, the Lion of the tribe of Juda, the Root of David, hath prevailed to open the book, and **to loose the seven seals** thereof.

6. And I beheld, and, lo, in the midst of the throne and of the four beasts, and in the midst of the elders, stood a Lamb as it had been slain, having seven horns and seven eyes, **which are the seven Spirits of Yahweh** sent forth into all the earth

2 Corinthians 1:21-2

21. Now he which established us with you in the Messiah, and hath **anointed us**, **is Yahweh.**

22. Who **hath also sealed us**, and given the earnest of the Spirit in our hearts

Ephesians 4:30 And grieve not the Spirit of Yahweh, whereby ye are sealed unto the day of redemption Romans 8:14-16

14. So then they that are in the flesh cannot please Yahweh.

15. **For ye have not received the spirit of bondage again to fear**; but <u>ye have received the Spirit of adoption</u>, whereby we cry, Abba, Father.

16. **The Spirit itself beareth witness with our Spirit**, that **we are the children of Yahweh.**

Romans 8:8-9

8.   So then they that are in the flesh cannot please Yahweh

9.   But **ye are not in the flesh, but in the Spirit, if so be that the Spirit of Yahweh dwell in you**. Now <u>if any man has not the Spirit of Yahweh, he is none of his</u>.

Romans 8:11 <u>**But if the Spirit of Him that raised up Immanuel from the dead dwell in you, he that raised up the Messiah from the dead shall also quicken your mortal bodies by his Spirit that dwelleth in you.**</u>

2 Corinthians 13:5 <u>Examine yourselves, whether ye be in the faith; prove your own selves. Know ye not your own selves, how that Yahweh the Messiah is in you, except ye be reprobates.</u>

Yahweh's Spirit is HIS seal.

Some teach the Sabbath is the Seal, but if that were the case, the whole 10 commandments would have to be.

If you break one, you break them all.

Ezekiel 36:27 <u>And I will put my Spirit within you, and cause you to walk in my statutes, and ye shall keep my judgments, and do them.</u>

E. THE ELECT ALL TAUGHT THE SAME THING:

This can only be done with Yahweh's Spirit infilling of the elect.

1 **Corinthians 1:10** Now I beseech you, brethren, by the name of Yahweh Messiah, that ye all speak the same thing, and that there be no divisions among you; but that ye be perfectly joined together in the same mind and in the same judgment.

2 **Corinthians 13:11** Finally, brethren, farewell. Be perfect, be of good comfort, be of one mind, live in peace; and Yahweh of love and peace shall be with you.

Galatians 1:6-8

6. I marvel that ye are so soon removed from him that called you into the faith of Yahweh unto another word:

7. Which is not another, but there be some that trouble you, and would pervert the Word of Yahweh.

8. **But though we, or a Messenger from heaven, teach any other Word unto you than that which we have taught unto you, let him be accursed.**

Acts 4:32-32

32. **And <u>the multitude of them that believed were of one heart and of one soul: neither said any of them that ought of the things which he possessed was his own, but they had all things common.</u>**

33. **And with great power gave the apostles witness of the resurrection of Yahweh's Spirit was upon them all.**

34. **Neither was there any among them that lacked: for as many as were possessors of lands or houses sold them, and brought the prices of the things that were sold.**

35 **And laid them down at the apostles' feet: and distribution was made unto every man according as he had need.**

CHAPTER 11

THE DIFFERENCE OF PRINCE AND KING AND ALSO LORD OUR GOD AND LORD YOUR GOD:

This study is to prove that where PRINCE is in these scriptures, the word KING goes. A KING rules over a KINGDOM, not a PRINCE. A KING makes the decision of war or peace, not a PRINCE.

Daniel 10:13 But the **prince / KING** of the kingdom of Persia withstood me one and twenty days: but, lo, Michael, one of the chief princes/**Messengers**, came to help me; and I remained there with the kings of Persia.

Isaiah 9:6 For unto us a child is born, unto us a son is given: and the government shall be upon his shoulder: and his name shall be called Wonderful, Counsellor, The Mighty YAHWEH, The everlasting Father, **The Prince / KING of Peace**

Revelation 19:16 On his robe and on his thigh, he has this name written: **King of kings (and Lord of lords. WAS ADDED.)**

Daniel 8:25 And through his policy also he shall cause craft to prosper in his hand; and he shall magnify himself in his heart, and by peace shall destroy many: he shall also stand up against the **prince of princes / King of kings**; but he shall be broken without hand.

With this Revelation 19:16 verse, King of kings is above all. Why would they put lord of lords if lord supposedly just meant master? A king is above all masters. That's why I truly believe that ("lord of lords" = /WAS added.)

1 Timothy 6:14-15

¹⁴ That thou keep this commandment without spot, unrebukable, until the appearing of our Master Yahweh Messiah:

¹⁵ Which in his times he shall shew, who is the blessed and only Potentate, the King of kings, and Lord of lords;

Revelation 17:14 These shall make war with the Lamb, and the Lamb shall overcome them: for he is **Lord of lords, and King of kings**: and they that are with him are called, and chosen, and faithful.

Psalm 136:3 O give thanks to the **Lord of lords**: for his mercy endureth forever.

Seems King of kings is much more fitting than Lord / Master of masters. Since a King is also the master of all.

Deuteronomy 10:17 For **the Lord / Yahweh** your God/deity/Almighty/Mighty One is **God of gods**, and **Lord of lords**, a great **God/deity/Mighty One**, a mighty, and a terrible, which regardeth not persons, nor taketh reward:

From the two verses below that follow Deuteronomy 10:17 prove there was no reason to say God of gods or Lord of lords because Yahweh said there were no other deities besides Him. But He would be the King of kings because of the earthly kings. Two main other verses prove that He is the only one and the only savior of the world.

Isaiah 45:5 I am **the LORD / Yahweh**, and **there is no other; apart from me there is no God/deity/Mighty One.** I will strengthen you, though you have not acknowledged **me**,

Isaiah 44:6-8 Thus saith **the LORD / Yahweh** the **King of Judaea,** and his redeemer **the LORD / Yahweh** of hosts; I am the first, and I am the last; and beside me **there is no God/deity/mighty one.**

Lord and God are sun deity names. These were put into scriptures by Constantine and his pagan bishops to make scriptures a lie and void of salvation.

There are a ton of scriptures that say, YAHWEH YOUR GOD / Mighty One. As a matter of fact, it repeats so many times in the scriptures it actually is annoying. I believe God was added to all these numerous scriptures to brainwash people with the word GOD. You would not realize how many Christians will tell you that His Name is GOD.

Deuteronomy 5:2,6,9,11,12,13,15,16,24,25,27,33,34 – I'm leaving in the pagan words since I am trying to bring out a point, not the truth, to the names.

² The **Lord OUR God** made a covenant with us in Horeb.

⁶ I am the **Lord your God**, who brought you out of the land of Egypt, out of the house of slavery.

⁹ You shall not bow down to them or serve them; for I the **Lord your God** am a jealous God, visiting the iniquity of the fathers on the children to the third and fourth generation of those who hate me,

¹¹ You shall not take the name of the **Lord your God** in vain, for the Lord will not hold him guiltless who takes his name in vain.

¹² Observe the Sabbath day, to keep it holy, as the **Lord your God** commanded you.

¹³ Six days you shall labor and do all your work, ¹⁴ but the seventh day is a Sabbath to the **Lord your God**.

¹⁵ You shall remember that you were a slave[c] in the land of Egypt, and the **Lord your God** brought you out from there with a mighty hand and an outstretched arm. Therefore, the **Lord your God** commanded you to keep the Sabbath day.

¹⁶ Honor your father and your mother, as the **Lord your God** commanded you, that your days may be long, and that it may go well with you in the land that the **Lord your God** is giving you.

²⁴ And ye said, Behold, the **Lord OUR God** hath shewed us his glory and his greatness, and we have heard his voice out of the midst of the fire: we have seen this day that God doth talk with man, and he liveth.

²⁵ Now therefore why should we die? For this great fire will consume us: if we hear the voice of the **Lord OUR God** anymore, then we shall die.

²⁷ Go thou near, and hear all that the **Lord OUR God** shall say: and speak thou unto us all that the **Lord OUR God** shall speak unto thee; and we will hear it, and do it.

³² Ye shall observe to do therefore as the **Lord your God** hath commanded you: ye shall not turn aside to the right hand or to the left.

³³ Ye shall walk in all the ways which the **Lord your God** hath commanded you, that ye may live, and that it may be well with you, and that ye may prolong your days in the land which ye shall possess.

In Deuteronomy, chapter 5. There are 11, **Lord your God,** and 5, **Lord our God**. That is 16, telling you the same thing over and over from a chapter with 33 verses, and 13 of them have one or more in each of those verses. Come on people, don't you think they knew who Yahweh was without being told constantly that He was the Almighty? Seriously, you will end up with a headache. All those are just from one chapter. Do you realize how many would be in all the books?

According to Strong's Concordance index of the Bible, the word 'God' is used **4,473 times** in the King James Version. However, this number may vary slightly depending on the Bible version and translation. The word 'God' is also one of the most common nouns in the Bible, along with 'LORD.'

WHEN A PERSON USES LORD AND GOD, THEY PROMOTE UNIVERSALISM!

CHAPTER 12

NO ONE HAS YAHWEH'S SPIRIT INFILLING:

THE FOLLOWING IS A TEST FOR ANYONE WHO SAYS THEY DO OR THINK THAT THEY DO. EVERYONE WILL FLUNK THE TEST:

No one can keep the Commandments without Yahweh's Spirit infilling.

1 John 3:24 And he that keepeth His commandments dwelleth in Him, and He in him. And hereby we know that He abideth in us, by the Spirit which He hath given us.

Ezekiel 36:27 And I will put My Spirit within you and cause you to walk in my statutes, and ye shall keep my judgments and do them.

Romans 8:9 But ye are not in the flesh, but in the Spirit, if so be that the Spirit of Yahweh dwell in you. Now if any <u>have not the Spirit of Yahweh, he is none of His.</u>

2 Corinthians 13:5 Examine yourselves to see whether you are in the faith; test yourselves. Do you not realize that Messiah Yahweh is in you unless, of course, you fail the test?

THE TEST:

1. In HIS name shall they cast out Satan. - This was also proven throughout the scriptures.

2. They shall speak with new tongues. - A tongue that could only come from Yahweh, tongues understood by all languages, why the true believers did not need an interpreter when they were sent to teach the Word.

3. They shall take up serpents. - Paul proved this fact. Acts 28:3-6

4. If they drink any deadly thing, it shall not hurt them. - They tried to kill true believers with poisons.

5. They shall lay hands on the sick, and they shall (will) recover. - Not maybe, or might, but WILL, and they were, throughout the scriptures.

6. They needed no man to teach them. The Spirit taught them all things. No Spirit-filled person needed to go and listen to a teacher to teach them. They were teachers. Are you running to and fro, still trying to find the truth? Of course, you are.

7. They all knew that they would suffer persecution and would be killed.

8. Do all of you THINK you are Spirit-filled, and are you all teaching the same thing that the other so-called Spirit-filled people are teaching? Of course not.

9. Psalm 37:25

I <u>have been young, and now am old; yet have I not seen the righteous forsaken, nor his seed begging bread.</u> Have you always had your needs met and never went hungry or without? LIKE PEOPLE ARE DOING TODAY.

10. Isaiah 41:10 Fear not for I am with thee............. Do you live in fear?

"TRUE SALVATION"

There is no salvation for today.

The true Messiah is Yahweh.

That real truth will be taught.

Christianity is all for naught.

The Peace Plan brings Yahweh's truth.

The Mark of the Beast is sooth.

It's your choice you will choose,

One you win, the other you lose.

Those who have never heard,

The truth of Yahweh's Word,

The Millennium is for them,

All will to be taught by Him.

Then there will be no excuse

When Satan is at last let loose.

To deceive man one last time,

Against humanity, his final crime.

Salvation is with Yahweh's Spirit. Life

is what then you will inherit.

Without having His Spirit infilling,

You will be a lost soul for burning.

This is and has been Satan's world,

In his lies we have been hurled.

The darker this world seems to get,

All the more light that is being lit.

By Gary W. Stanfield

CHAPTER 13

THOSE BORN OF YAHWEH DO NOT TRANSGRESS

1 John 3:9

^{9.} <u>Whosoever is born of Yahweh doth not commit transgressions; for *His seed remaineth in him: and he cannot transgress, because he is born of Yahweh.*</u>

If Yahweh cannot transgress, then those with His Spirit in them cannot either, as long as they don't turn their back on Yahweh.

The following verses in Romans sum it all up. What a person without Yahweh's Spirit is, and those who did and will have Yahweh's Spirit.

Romans 8:1-17

<u>1. There is therefore now no condemnation to them which are in Messiah Yahweh, who walk not after the flesh, but after the Spirit.</u>

<u>2. For the law of the Spirit of life in Messiah Yahweh hath made me free from the law of transgression and death.</u>

<u>3. For what the law could not do, in that it was weak through the flesh, Yahweh sending his own Son in the likeness of transgression flesh, and for transgression, condemned transgression in the flesh:</u>

<u>4. That the righteousness of the law might be fulfilled in us, who walk not after the flesh, but after the Spirit.</u>

83

5. **For they that are after the flesh do mind the things of the flesh; but they that are after the Spirit the things of the Spirit.**

6. **For to be carnally minded is death; but to be spiritually minded is life and peace.**

7. **Because the carnal mind is enmity against Yahweh: for it is not subject to the law of Yahweh, neither indeed can be.**

8. **So then they that are in the flesh cannot please Yahweh.**

9. **But ye are not in the flesh, but in the Spirit, if so be that the Spirit of Yahweh dwell in you. Now if any man have not the Spirit of Yahweh, he is none of His.**

10. **And if Yahweh be in you, the body is dead because of transgression; but the Spirit is life because of righteousness.**

11. **But if the Spirit of Him that raised up Immanuel from the dead dwell in you, he that raised up the Messiah from the dead shall also quicken your mortal bodies by his Spirit that dwelleth in you.**

12. **Therefore, brethren, we are debtors, not to the flesh, to live after the flesh.**

13. **For if ye live after the flesh, ye shall die: but if ye through the Spirit do mortify the deeds of the body, ye shall live.**

14. **For as many as are led by the Spirit of Yahweh, they are the sons of Yahweh.**

15. **For ye have not received the spirit of bondage again to fear; but ye have received the Spirit of adoption, whereby we cry, Abba, Father.**

16. **The Spirit itself beareth witness with our spirit, that we are the children of Yahweh:**

17. And if children, then heirs; heirs of Yahweh, and joint-heirs with Messiah; if so be that we suffer with him, that we may be also esteemed together.

CHAPTER 14

THE BOOK OF ACTS, THE FIRST 15 CHAPTERS, MINUS THE FIRST ONE.

DAY OF PENTECOST: WHERE IS THIS GOING ON TODAY?

NOWHERE.

Keep in mind this was to the Jews only at this time. Acts Chapter 2 tells us about the day of Pentecost when Yahweh's Spirit was poured out. Acts 2:5-6 tells us there were Jews, devout men, out of every nation under heaven. Every man heard them speak in their own language. Acts 2:41 tells us that [they that received his Word] were baptized and added about 3,000 souls. Acts 2:43 tells us that fear came upon every soul, and many wonders and signs were done by the apostles. Acts 2:47 tells us that Yahweh added to the assembly daily, such as should be saved.

A LAME MAN HEALED:

Acts 3:2-10 tells us of a certain man who was lame from his mother's womb and laid daily at the gate of the House of Yahweh asking for alms. When Peter and John were passing by, he asked for alms from them, and Peter told him, "Silver and gold have I none, but such as I have I give to thee." Then he was healed and he went walking and leaping, praising Yahweh. The people who saw him were amazed to see what had happened to him. Acts Chapter 4:1-3 tells us the priests and the captain of the House of Yahweh, and the Sadducees, came upon Peter and John and imprisoned

them. Acts 4:4 tells us that many of them that [heard the word] believed, and the number of the men was about 5,000.

SOLOMON'S PORCH:

Acts 5:12 tells us that by the hands of the apostles were many signs and wonders worked among the people and they were all of one accord in Solomon's porch. And believers were the more added to Yahweh, multitudes both men and women.

Acts 5:15-16 tells us that they carried the sick into the streets and laid them on beds and couches. There also came together the multitude from other cities, bringing sick people and ones with unclean spirits. THEY WERE ALL HEALED. The priests and the Sadducees, filled with jealousy, laid hands upon the apostles and put them in prison again.

Acts 5:27-28 tells us that they went before the council, and the council said, "Did we not strictly tell you that you should not teach in this name?"

Acts 5:32 tells us that they were witnesses of these things and so was the Spirit that Yahweh had given to them that obey him.

Acts 5:41-42 tells us that they departed from the council, rejoicing that they were counted worthy to suffer dishonor for the name. [They ceased not to teach Yahweh as the Messiah.]

STEPHEN:

Acts 6:1 tells us that in these days the number of the disciples was multiplying.

Acts 6:7 tells us that [the word of Yahweh increased] and the number of the disciples multiplied in Zion greatly. Also, a great company of priests were obedient to the faith.

Acts 6:8 tells us that Stephen, full of the Spirit and power, worked great signs among the people.

Acts 7:59 tells us that when they stoned Stephen, he called upon Yahweh, saying receive my Spirit, and he fell asleep.

SAUL:

Acts 8:1, 3 & 4 tells us that Saul consented to Stephen's death, and also there arose a great persecution against the assembly which was in Zion, and they were scattered abroad throughout the regions of Judaea and Samaria. Saul made havoc upon the assembly, entering into every house and committing every man and woman to prison. [Those that were scattered abroad went everywhere teaching the word.]

Acts 9:31 tells us that the assembly had rest throughout all Judaea, Galilee and Samaria and walked in the fear of Yahweh and in the comfort of the Spirit were multiplied.

PHILIP:

Acts 8:5-7 tells us that [Philip taught the Messiah unto them] and the people were with one accord and gave heed unto those things which Philip spake hearing and seeing the miracles which he did: unclean spirits came out of many that were possessed, many with palsies, many that were lame were healed.

AENEAS HEALED:

Acts 9:32-35 tells us that Peter found a certain man named Aeneas, who was in bed for eight (8) years with palsy. He was healed and arose immediately, and ALL that dwelt at Lydda and Saron saw and turned to Yahweh.

CORNELIUS, BEGINNING OF GENTILE SALVATION:

Acts 10:2 tells us about Cornelius, a Gentile who feared Yahweh with all his house, and he prayed to Yahweh always. He had a vision of a Messenger of Yahweh appearing to him, who told him that his prayers and alms had come up for a memorial before Yahweh.

Acts 10:5 tells us that Cornelius was told to send for Simon Peter.

Acts 10:24-25 tells us that Cornelius and his kinsmen and near friends met Peter. [Peter taught them about salvation].

Acts 10:44 tells us that while Peter yet spoke, [the Spirit fell on all them which heard the word].

Acts 10:45 tells us that the Jews who were with Peter were all astonished because the Gentiles also poured out the gift of the Spirit.

Acts 11 tells us about Peter returning to Zion and telling the Jewish believers what had happened with the Gentiles.

Acts 11:18 tells us that they understood that Yahweh granted to the Gentiles repentance unto life.

Acts 11:19 tells us that those who were scattered abroad upon the persecution that arose about Stephen [taught the word to no one else but only to the Jews].

Acts 11:20 tells us that some of them were men of Cyprus and Cyrene, which [taught the Greeks].

Acts 11:21 tells us that the hand of Yahweh was with them and a great number believed and turned to Yahweh.

HEROD'S PERSECUTIONS:

Acts 12:1-5 tells us about King Herod persecuting certain believers. He killed James, the brother of John, with a sword. Seeing this pleased the Jews, he took Peter also and imprisoned him.

Acts 12:7-11 tells us about a Messenger of Yahweh who freed Peter.

Acts 12:19 tells us that Herod looked for Peter but could not find him. Acts 12:24 tells us that the [word of Yahweh grew] and multiplied.

PAUL AND BARNABAS:

Acts 13:44-49 tells us that on a Sabbath [came almost the whole city together to hear the word of Yahweh]. When the Jews saw the multitudes, they were filled with envy and spoke against the things which Paul said. Paul and Barnabas told them it was necessary that the word of Yahweh should first have been spoken to them, but since they did not accept it, they turned to the Gentiles. The Gentiles who heard this were glad and praised the word of Yahweh and as many as were ordained to eternal life believed.

Acts 13:50 tells us that the Jews stirred up the devout and honorable women and the chief men of the city and raised persecution against Paul and Barnabas and kicked them out.

Acts 14:1 tells us that [Paul and Barnabas went together into the House of Yahweh of the Jews and spoke] that a great multitude both of the Jews and of the Gentiles believed.

Acts 14:3 tells us they stayed there a long time [speaking boldly in Yahweh, giving testimony unto the word of his Spirit] and were granted signs and wonders to be done by their hands.

Acts 14:5 tells us they were going to be assaulted by Gentiles and Jews with their rulers to stone them, but they were aware of this and fled.

John 21:25 And there are also many other things which Immanuel did, the which, if they should be written every one, I suppose that even the world itself could not contain the books that should be written.

For one to prove the above verse, do you realize that every person that could not hear, retarded, and demon-possessed was all healed because everyone back then had to hear the truth, the whole truth, so they could believe that truth or not? This is also going to happen again during the 7Year Peace Plan after WW3.

CHAPTER 15

TRANSGRESSIONS AND THE SPIRIT INFILLING:

When and only when are you truly given salvation?

Ephesians 4:6,7,8; 11-16

6. One Yahweh and Father of all, who is above all, and through all, **and in you all**.

7. But unto every one of us is given the Spirit according to the measure of the gift of Yahweh.

8. Wherefore He saith, When He ascended on high, He led captivity captive and gave gifts unto men.

11. And He gave some, apostles; and some, prophets; and some teachers

12. **For the perfecting of the believers, for the work of the ministry/assembly, for the edifying of the body of Yahweh:**

13. **Till we all come in the unity of the Faith, and of the knowledge of the Son of Yahweh**, unto **a perfect man, unto the measure of the stature of the fulness of Yahweh:**

14. **That we henceforth be no more children, tossed to and fro, and carried about with every wind of doctrine, by the sleight of men, and cunning craftiness, whereby they lie in wait to deceive;**

15. But speaking the truth in love, may grow up into Him in all things, which is the head, even Yahweh:

16. From whom the whole body fitly joined together and compacted by that which every joint supplieth, according to the effectual working in the measure of every part, maketh increase of the body unto the edifying of itself in love.

In other words, when you first believe, you become a believer, but you are not Spirit-filled yet. So, the Spirit-filled believers were the ones who taught the new believers in Yahweh Messiah until Yahweh saw fit to fill them with His Spirit. The Spirit-filled people were taught by the Spirit and knew all things. The believers who were not Spirit-filled had to be taught of Yahweh's ways.

Salvation is when you are filled with Yahweh's Spirit and not before.

They did not have salvation when they asked for forgiveness or when they were baptized in His Name, Yahweh. So, they were not so-called saved at that time.

Let me explain what the scriptures really teach: At the time of repentance, asking for forgiveness of transgressions is the first step to salvation. The person became an Apprentice for the infilling of Yahweh's Spirit, and Yahweh started helping them clean themselves up; at baptism, this was the second step to salvation, and they became a Candidate for the infilling of Yahweh's Spirit. This is when the person was thriving to serve Yahweh and Yahweh is still helping them to clean themselves up, so His Spirit can dwell in them. When this was done, they became a Journeyman, which was the third and last step to truly believing, and that is when the Master Yahweh filled the people with His Spirit, and this was a true believer in Yahweh.

Acts 5:32

32 And we are His witnesses of these things; and so is also **the Spirit, whom Yahweh hath given to them that obey Him.**

John 7:39

[39] (*__But this spake he of the Spirit, which they that believed on him should receive__*: for the Spirit was not yet given; because Immanuel was not yet esteemed.

Acts 1:8

[8] But __ye shall receive power, after that the Spirit has come upon you: and ye shall be witnesses unto me__ both in Zion, and in all Judaea, and in Samaria, and unto the uttermost part of the earth.

Hebrews 2:3,4

[3.] How shall we escape, if we neglect so great salvation; which at the first began to be spoken by the Master and was confirmed unto us by them that heard him.

[4.] __Yahweh also bearing them witness, both with signs and wonders, and with diver's miracles, and gifts of the Spirit, according to His own will?__

Luke 10:19

[19] Behold, __I give unto you the power to tread on serpents and scorpions, and over all the power of the enemy: and nothing shall by any means hurt you.__

__NOTE:__ **As you should be able to see, Christians do not have Yahweh's Spirit, nor do the so-called Pentecostals. In fact, no one today has Yahweh's Spirit infilling.**

Romans 8:9

[9] But ye are not in the flesh but in the Spirit. If so, be the Spirit of Yahweh dwells in you. **Now if any man has not the Spirit of Yahweh, he is none of**

His.

2 Cor. 13:5

[5] Examine yourselves, whether ye be in the faith; prove your own selves. **Know ye not your own selves, how that Yahweh Messiah is in you, except ye be reprobates?**

CHAPTER 16

THE ROMAN EMPIRE RULED THE INHABITED PART OF THE EARTH.

Showing different translations with how they brought about their version of the same verse.

New American Standard Bible (NASB)

Luke 2:1 Now in those days a decree went out from Caesar Augustus, that <u>THAT A CENSUS BE TAKEN IN ALL THE INHABITED EARTH.</u>

<u>New Living Translation (NLT)</u>

Luke 2:1. At that time, the Roman emperor, Augustus, decreed that <u>A CENSUS SHOULD BE TAKEN THROUGHOUT THE ROMAN EMPIRE.</u>

Wycliffe Bible (WYC)

Luke 2:1 And it was done in those days, a commandment went out from the emperor Augustus [a commandment went out from Caesar Augustus], <u>THAT ALL THE WORLD SHOULD BE DESCRIBED.</u>

World English Bible (WEB)

Luke 2:1 Now in those days, a decree went out from Caesar Augustus <u>THAT ALL THE WORLD SHOULD BE ENROLLED.</u>

New Revised Standard Version Catholic Edition (NRSVCE)

Luke 2:1 In those days a decree went out from Emperor Augustus THAT ALL THE WORLD SHOULD BE REGISTERED.

1599 Geneva Bible (GNV)

Luke 2:1 And it came to pass in those days, that there came a decree from Augustus Caesar, THAT ALL THE WORLD SHOULD BE TAXED.

King James

Luke 2:1 And it came to pass in those days, that there went out a decree from Caesar Augustus that ALL THE WORLD SHOULD BE TAXED.

From the above verses, people should be able to see that the Roman Empire engulfed all the people that inhabited the earth at that time.

Knowing this, you will now understand how Yahweh's Elect went to the ends of the world. The Roman Empire was the world to humanity.

Revelation 6:8 And I looked, and behold a pale horse: and his name that sat on him was

Death and the grave followed with him (Satan). And power was given unto them (Emperors) OVER THE FOURTH PART OF THE EARTH, to kill with sword, and with hunger, and with death, and with the beasts of the earth.

Every person, including children suspected of being of the faith in Yahweh, were killed without recourse to laws or by any other means. Horsemen rode across the empire with a public proclamation of extermination.

When the armies of Rome surrounded and then destroyed Zion and tore the House of Yahweh down, that's when the Jews headed for the mountains. The believing Gentiles did, too.

Ezekiel 5:12 A third part of thee shall die with the pestilence, and with famine shall they be consumed in the midst of thee: and <u>a third part shall fall by the sword round about thee, and I will scatter a third part into all the winds, and I will draw out a sword after them.</u>

Daniel 9:7 O Yahweh, righteousness belongeth unto thee, but unto us confusion of faces, as at this day; to the men of Judah, and to the inhabitants of Zion, and unto all Judaea, that are near, and that are far off, through all the countries whither thou hast driven them, because of their trespass that they have trespassed against thee.

Ezekiel 20:23 I lifted mine hand unto them also in the wilderness, that I would scatter them among the heathen, and disperse them through the countries; The First Persecution, Under Nero, 67 C.E., Zion destroyed in 70 C.E.

Luke 21:20-24

20 And when ye shall see Zion compassed with armies, then know that the desolation thereof is nigh.

21 Then let them which are in Judaea flee to the mountains; and let them which are in the midst of it depart out; and let not them that are in the countries enter herein.

22 <u>For these be the days of vengeance, that all things which are written may be fulfilled.</u>

23 But woe unto them that are with child, and to them that give suck, in those days! For there shall be great distress in the land and wrath upon this people.

24 And they shall fall by the edge of the sword and shall be led away captive into all nations: and Zion shall be trodden down of the Gentiles, until the times of the Gentiles be fulfilled.

Read about and study the Christian Crusades, how the Christians were fighting the Muslims while also killing the Jews and persecuting them, and then the Christians breaking away from the Papacy authority, which also caused Christians to kill Christians before the Crusades were over with. Satan is all about death.

NOW FOR THE TEACHING OF YAHWEH'S WORD TO THE WORLD BACK THEN AND WHEN THE FORMER RAIN OF YAHWEH'S SPIRIT WAS POURED OUT:

He then told them to wait in Zion until the promise of the Father, which was the infilling of the Spirit of Yahweh in them. He also told them once this happens go and teach the Word to every creature on earth.

He told them those who believe and are baptized (IN HIS SPIRIT) will be saved, and those who believe not will be condemned. THIS WAS FOR THOSE BACK THEN.

Matthew 28:15-18

15. And he said unto them, go ye into all the world, and teach the Word to every creature.

16. He that believeth and is baptized shall be saved; but he that believeth not shall be damned.

17. And these signs shall follow them that believe; In My Name (Yahweh) shall they cast out devils; they shall speak with new tongues;

18. They shall take up serpents; and if they drink any deadly thing, it shall not hurt them; they shall recover.

Mark 16:15 <u>Go ye into all the world and preach/teach the Word to every creature.</u>

THEY WENT TO THE KNOWN POPULATED WORLD, WITHIN THE ROMAN EMPIRE.

Matthew 28:19 Go ye, therefore, and teach all nations, baptizing them in the name of the Father, and of the Son, and of the Spirit. (Yahweh)

Luke 10:19 Behold, I give unto you power to tread on serpents and scorpions, and over all the power of the enemy: and nothing shall by any means hurt you.

Luke 24:47-51

47. And that repentance and remission of transgressions should be taught in His Name (Yahweh) among all nations, beginning at Zion.

48. And ye are witnesses of these things.

49. And behold, I send the promise of my Father upon you: but tarry ye in the city of Zion, until ye be endued with power from on high.

50. And he led them out as far as to Bethany, and he lifted his hands, and blessed them.

51. And it came to pass, while he blessed them, he was parted from them and carried up into heaven.

Galatians 1:11, 12

12. For I neither received it of man, neither was I taught it, but by the revelation of Yahweh Messiah.

1 Corinthians 1:17 For the Messiah sent me not to baptize, but to teach the Word: not with wisdom of words, lest the Spirit of Yahweh should be made of none effect.

1 Corinthians 2:1 And so it was with me, brothers and sisters. When I came to you, I did not come with eloquence or human wisdom as I proclaimed to you the testimony about Yahweh.

1 Corinthians 2:4,5,7,8,10-13

4. <u>And my speech and my teaching were not with enticing words of man's wisdom but in DEMONSTRATION of the SPIRIT and of POWER.</u>

5. <u>That your faith should not stand in the wisdom of men, but in the power of Yahweh.</u> 7. But we speak the wisdom of Yahweh in a mystery, even the hidden wisdom, which Yahweh ordained before the world unto His righteousness.

8. Which none of the Kings of this world knew: for had they known it, they would not have impaled/killed Yahweh of majesty.

[10.] But Yahweh hath revealed them unto us by His Spirit: for the Spirit searches all things, yea, the deep things of Yahweh.

[11.] For what man knows the things of a man, save the spirit of man which is in him? Even so, the things of Yahweh knows no man, but the Spirit of Yahweh.

[12.] Now we have received, not the spirit of the world, but the Spirit which is of Yahweh; that we might know the things that are freely given to us of Yahweh.

[13.] Which things also we speak, not in the words which man's wisdom teaches, but which the Spirit teaches; comparing spiritual things with spiritual.

Ephesians 1:2 Blessings be to you, and peace, from Yahweh our Father, and from the Master Yahweh Messiah.

CHAPTER 17

A. TRUTH WAS TAUGHT TO EVERY PERSON IN THE DAYS OF PETER AND PAUL - THE FULFILLMENT:

Mark 16:15 And he said unto them, go ye into all the world, and preach/**teach the Word to every creature.**

Mark 16:20 And they went forth, and preached/taught everywhere, Yahweh working with them, and confirming the word with signs following.

Luke 4:18 The Spirit of Yahweh is upon me, because He hath anointed me to teach the Word to the poor; he hath sent me to heal the brokenhearted, to teach deliverance to the captives, and recovering of sight to the blind, to set at liberty them that are bruised,

Acts 8:4 Therefore they that were scattered abroad went everywhere teaching the Word.

Romans 1:5 By whom we have received power and apostleship, for obedience to the faith among all nations, for his name:

Romans 10:18 Their sound went into all the earth, and their words unto the ends of the world.

The above verse makes it sound like the whole earth was populated when it was not. The Roman Empire engulfed the whole of humanity when Constantine ruled the Roman Empire. It means the populated part of the world and earth at that time.

According to the commandment of the everlasting Yahweh, made known to all nations for the obedience of faith:

Colossians 1:23 If ye continue in the faith grounded and settled,

Mark 13:10 and be not moved away from the hope of the word, which ye have heard, and which was taught to every creature which is under heaven; whereof I Paul am made a teacher.

Colossians 1: 5, 6

5.Ye heard the Word of truth.

6. which comes unto you, as *it is* in all the world; and bringeth forth fruit, as *it doth* also in you, since the day ye heard *of it*, and knew the Spirit of Yahweh in truth.

Acts 17:6 And when they found them not, they drew Jason and certain brethren unto the rulers of the city, crying, these that have turned the world upside down have come hither also;

Romans 1:5 By whom we have received faith and apostleship, for obedience to the faith among all nations, for his name:

Romans 1:8 First, I thank Yahweh through Yahweh Messiah for you all, that your faith is spoken of throughout the whole world.

2 Thessalonians 2:13 But we are bound to give thanks always to Yahweh for you, brethren beloved of Yahweh, because Yahweh hath from the beginning chosen you to salvation through infilling of the Spirit and belief of the truth:

Titus 2:11 For Spirit of Yahweh that brings salvation hath appeared to all men.

(THAT HAPPENED BACK THEN AND WILL HAPPEN AGAIN IN THE FUTURE)

Matthew 24:14 <u>**And this Word of the kingdom shall be preached/taught in all the world**</u> <u>for a witness unto all nations; and then shall the end come.</u>

THIS VERSE IS THE WHOLE WORLD; WE KNOW THIS BECAUSE IT IS TAUGHT TO ALL NATIONS JUST BEFORE THE END.

B. THE TRIBULATION PERIOD FOR THOSE BACK THEN BROKE OUT, AND ALL BELIEVERS IN YAHWEH MESSIAH ENDED UP BEING KILLED OFF:

NOTE: There were Great Tribulations and Persecutions that broke out at this time against the elect after the Spirit was given. This same thing will happen again after Yahweh pours His Spirit out during the Papacy's 7-Year Peace Plan.

Acts 14:22 Confirming the souls of the disciples and exhorting them to continue in the faith, and that we must, through much tribulation, enter into the kingdom of Yahweh.

The 4th Seal represents the Roman Empire and the 11   Emperor persecutions that killed off all the last of the elect of Yahweh at that time.

Revelation 6:8 And I looked and behold a pale horse: and his name that sat on him was Death, and the grave followed with him (SATAN). And power was given unto them (Emperors) over the fourth part of the earth, to kill with sword, and with hunger, and with death, and with the beasts of the earth**.**

Revelation 12:12 Therefore rejoice, ye heavens, and ye that dwell in them. Woe to the inhibiters of the earth and of the sea! for the devil has come down unto you, having great wrath, because he knows that he hath but a short time.

NOTE: Satan came when the Messiah went back to heaven and kicked him out to this earth for good.

Revelation 12:11 And they overcame him (SATAN) by the blood of the Lamb, and by the word of their testimony; and they loved not their lives unto the death.

C. THEY WERE ALL PERSECUTED THAT BELIEVED IN YAHWEH MESSIAH:

The persecutions happening within Christianity in many of the countries today are for to deceive the Christians into thinking they are true believers and why they are being persecuted and killed. It will be the Christians when it becomes a One World Religion that will kill and persecute those who believe in Yahweh Messiah.

Acts 14:22 Confirming the souls of the disciples, and exhorting them to continue in the faith, and that we must through much tribulation enter into the kingdom of Yahweh.

2 Timothy 3:12 Yea, and all that will live righteously in Messiah Yahweh shall suffer persecution.

Acts 9:16 "For I (Yahweh) will show him how much he must suffer for My name's sake."

Romans 8:17 And if children, heirs also, heirs of Yahweh and fellow heirs with Messiah, if indeed we suffer with Him so that we may also be esteemed with Him.

Philippians 1:29 For unto you it is given on the behalf of Yahweh, not only to believe on Him, but also to suffer for His sake;

Romans 8:35-39

[35.] Who shall separate us from the love of Yahweh? shall tribulation, or distress, or persecution, or famine, or nakedness, or peril, or sword?

[36.] As it is written, for thy sake we are killed all day long; we are accounted as sheep for the slaughter.

[37.] Nay, in all these things we are more than conquerors through him that loved us.

[38.] For I am persuaded, that neither death, nor life, nor angels, nor principalities, nor powers, nor things present, nor things to come,38. Nor height, nor depth, nor any other creature, shall be able to separate us from the love of Yahweh, which is in Messiah Yahweh our Master.

Romans 8:36 Just as it is written, "FOR YOUR SAKE WE ARE BEING PUT TO DEATH ALL DAY LONG; WE WERE CONSIDERED AS SHEEP TO BE SLAUGHTERED.

Acts 20:29-30

[29.] For I know this, that after my departing shall grievous wolves enter in among you, not sparing the flock.

[30.] Also of your own selves shall men arise, speaking perverse things, to draw away disciples after them.

2 Peter 2:2-3

[1.] But there were false prophets also among the people, even as there shall be false teachers among you, who privily shall bring in damnable heresies, even denying Yahweh that bought them, and bring upon themselves swift destruction.

2. And many shall follow their pernicious ways; by reason of whom the way of truth shall be evil spoken of.

3 And through covetousness shall they with feigned words make merchandise of you: whose judgment now of a long time lingereth not, and their damnation slumbereth not.

1 John 2:18 Little children, it is the last time: and as ye have heard that anti-Messiah shall come, even now are there many anti-Messiahs; whereby we know that it is the last time.

1 John 4:4 Ye are of Yahweh, little children, and have overcome them: because greater is HE THAT IS IN YOU, than he that is in the world.

They received the Former Rain of Yahweh's Spirit. After the elect were all killed off, then this became Satan's world because it was our ancestors who did not believe at that time. The opening of the 5th Seal shows them all dead under the table, asking Yahweh how long before He avenges their blood. Yahweh tells them to wait a little season until their fellow brethren like them should be killed.

Revelation 6:9-11

9. And when he had opened the fifth seal, I saw under the altar the souls of them that were slain for the Word of Yahweh, and for the testimony which they held:

10. And they cried with a loud voice, saying, how long, O Yahweh, righteous and true, dost thou not judge and avenge our blood on them that dwell on the earth?

11 And white robes were given unto every one of them; and it was said unto them, that they should rest yet for a little season, until their fellow servants also and their brethren, that should be killed as they were, should be fulfilled.

2 Timothy 1:12 For the which cause I also suffer these things: nevertheless, I am not ashamed: for I know whom I have believed and am persuaded that He is able to keep that which I have committed unto Him against that day.

The Roman Empire (4th Seal)

"And I looked, and behold a pale horse: and his name that sat on him was Death (Emperor), and the grave followed with him. And power was given unto THEM {Emperors} over the fourth part of the earth, to kill with sword, and with hunger, and with death, and with the beasts of the earth."

"And they overcame him {Emperor} by the blood of the Lamb, and by the word of their testimony; for they loved not their lives even unto their death." This was done by the eleven Roman persecutions until the last one took their last breath. They all were laid to rest, and each and everyone was surely blessed.

Many died horrible deaths, thrown to lions, impaled, killed by gladiators, alive were they burned. Their souls with everlasting life were for what they yearned for. So, for their testimony to prove that Yahweh was true, they had to die and this they knew. By the Spirit, they were brave. Now, they are all in the grave.

These are those under the table that Yahweh told "to rest" till those like them will be killed and will also pass the test. His future Peace Plan people, the Anti-Messiah, will not deceive. Then, after this, they shall all be redeemed, and Yahweh's wrath on those that did not in Him believe.

By Gary Wendell Stanfield

Revelation 12:11 And they overcame him by the blood of the Lamb, and by the word of their testimony; and they loved not their lives unto the death.

10 Roman Emperor Persecutions from 54 C.E. to 305 C.E. Lasted for 251 years.

Constantine came into power in 306 C.E. He had the 11ᵗʰ one that lasted until 312 or 313.

D. DOES YAHWEH HEAR ANYONE'S PRAYERS TODAY SINCE THE ELECT WERE ALL KILLED OFF?

There is no salvation for today, so Yahweh does not hear anyone's prayers because no one today has His Spirit infilling. His ears are only opened to the righteous, His Elect when the time of salvation comes once again during the 7Year Peace Plan after WW3. This is and has been Satan's world.

2 Corinthians 13:5 Examine yourselves, whether ye be in the faith; prove your own selves. Know ye not your own selves, how that Yahweh Messiah is in you, except ye be reprobates?

No one today has Yahweh's Spirit infilling, and that fact is proven by the scriptures. This whole world today is a bunch of reprobates without salvation.

Proverbs 15:29 Yahweh is far from the wicked, but He heareth the prayer of the righteous.

John 9:31 Now we know that Yahweh heareth not transgressors, but if any man be a worshiper of Yahweh, and doeth his will, him he will hear.

Psalms 34:1-22

¹· I will bless Yahweh at all times: His praise shall continually be in my mouth.

2. My soul shall make her boast in Yahweh: the humble shall hear thereof and be glad.

3. O magnify Yahweh with me and let us exalt His name together.

4. <u>I sought Yahweh, and He heard me, and delivered me from all my fears.</u>

5. They looked unto Him and were lightened: and their faces were not ashamed.

6. <u>This poor man cried, and Yahweh heard him, and saved him out of all his troubles.</u>

7. <u>The Messenger of Yahweh encampeth round about them that fear Him, and delivereth them.</u>

8. O taste and see that Yahweh is good: blessed is the man that trusteth in Him.

9. O fear Yahweh, ye His upright: for there is no want to them that fear Him.

10. The young lions do lack and suffer hunger: but they that seek Yahweh shall not want any good thing.

11. Come, ye children, hearken unto Me: I will teach you the fear of Yahweh.

12. What man is he that desireth life, and loveth many days, that he may see good?

13. Keep thy tongue from evil, and thy lips from speaking guile.

14. Depart from evil, and do good; seek peace, and pursue it.

15. <u>The eyes of Yahweh are upon the righteous, and his ears are open unto their cry.</u>

16. <u>The face of Yahweh is against them that do evil, to cut off the remembrance of them from the earth.</u>

17. <u>The righteous cry, and Yahweh heareth, and delivereth them out of all their troubles.</u>

^{18.} Yahweh is nigh unto them that are of a broken heart; and saveth such as be of a contrite spirit.

^{19.} Many are the afflictions of the righteous: but Yahweh delivereth him out of them all.

^{20.} He keepeth all his bones: not one of them is broken.

^{21.} Evil shall slay the wicked: and they that hate the righteous shall be desolate.

^{22.} Yahweh redeemeth the soul of His servants: and none of them that trust in Him shall be desolate.

Yahweh only hears the prayers of the righteous. There are none today.

The verses below were when salvation was still attainable.

Isaiah 59:2 But <u>your iniquities have separated you and Yahweh, and your transgressions have hid his face from you, that he will not hear.</u>

Psalms 66:18 If <u>I regard iniquity in my heart, Yahweh will not hear me:</u>

Acts 3:19 Repent ye therefore, and be converted, that your transgressions may be blotted out, when the times of refreshing shall come from the presence of Yahweh;

Isaiah 55:6-7

^{6.} <u>Seek ye Yahweh while he may be found, call ye upon him while he is near.</u>

^{7.} <u>Let the wicked forsake his way, and the unrighteous man his thoughts: and let him return unto Yahweh, and he will have mercy upon him; for he will abundantly pardon.</u>

Matthew 7:7-11

8. Ask, and it shall be given you; seek, and ye shall find; knock, and it shall be opened unto you:

9. For everyone that asketh receiveth; and he that seeketh findeth; and to him that knocketh it shall be opened.

10. Or what man is there of you, whom if his son ask bread, will he give him a stone?

11. Or if he asks a fish, will he give him a serpent?

12. If ye then, being evil, know how to give good gifts unto your children, how much more shall your Father which is in heaven give good things to them that ask him?

Mark 11:23-24

23 For verily I say unto you, That whosoever shall say unto this mountain, Be thou removed, and be thou cast into the sea; and shall not doubt in his heart, but shall believe that those things which he saith shall come to pass; he shall have whatsoever he saith.

24 Therefore, I say unto you, what things soever ye desire, when ye pray, believe that ye receive them, and ye shall have them

John 14:12-14

12. Verily, verily, I say unto you, he that believeth on Me, the works that I do shall he do also; and greater works than these shall he do; because I go unto my Father.

13. And whatsoever ye shall ask in My Name, that will I do, that the Father may be esteemed in the Son.

14 If ye shall ask any thing in My Name, I will do it.

1 John 5:14-15

14. And this is the confidence that we have in Him, that, if we ask any thing according to

His will, He heareth us:

15. And if we know that He hear us, whatsoever we ask, we know that we have the petitions that we desired of Him.

E. THE GREAT FALLING AWAY AND THE REVEALING OF THE MAN OF TRANSGRESSION:

2 Thessalonians 2:1-16

1. Now we beseech you, brethren, by the coming of our Master Yahweh Messiah, and by our gathering together unto Him,

2. That ye be not soon shaken in mind, or be troubled, neither by spirit, nor by word, nor by letter as from us, as that the day of Yahweh is at hand.

3. Let no man deceive you in any wise; for, except the falling away come first, and the 'man of transgression' be revealed the 'son of perdition',

4. He that opposes and exalts himself (POPE) against all that is called a deity (#666) or that is worshiped; so that he sits in the Temple of God /deity, setting himself forth as a deity. 5. Don't you remember, that, when I was yet with you, I told you these things?

6. And now you know that which restrains, to the end that he (Pontifex Maximus) may be revealed in his own season.

7. For the mystery of lawlessness already works, only there is one that restrains now (Emperor), until he be taken out of the way.

8. And then shall that Wicked be revealed, whom Yahweh shall consume with the spirit of his mouth and shall destroy with the brightness of His coming: 9.

Even him (POPE), who's coming is after the working of **Satan with all power and signs and lying wonders,**

¹⁰· And with all deceivableness of unrighteousness in them that perish; because they received not the love of the truth, that they might be saved.

¹¹· And for this cause Yahweh shall send them strong delusion, that they should believe a lie:

¹²· That they all might be damned who believed not the truth but had pleasure in unrighteousness.

¹³· But we are bound to give thanks always to Yahweh for you, brethren beloved of Yahweh, because Yahweh hath from the beginning chosen you to salvation through righteousness of the Spirit and belief of the truth:

¹⁴· Whereunto he called you by our word, to the obtaining of the righteousness of our Master Yahweh Messiah.

¹⁵· Therefore, brethren, stand fast, and hold the teachings which ye have been taught, whether by word, or our letter.

¹⁶· Now our Master Yahweh Messiah Himself, and Yahweh, even our Father, which hath loved us, and hath given us everlasting consolation and good hope through righteousness,

1 John 2:18 Little children, it is the last time: and as ye have heard that anti-Messiah shall come, even now are there many anti-Messiahs; whereby we know that it is the last time.

CHAPTER 18

FORMER AND LATTER RAIN:

The outpouring of Yahweh's Spirit. There was a Former Rain, and there will be a Latter Rain. <u>The Former Rain was poured out starting at Pentecost,</u> and the true believers were killed off for their testimony that Yahweh was true.

JAMES 5:7

<u>Be patient therefore, brethren, unto the coming of Yahweh.</u> Behold, <u>the husbandman waiteth for the precious fruit of the earth, and hath long patience for it</u>, **until he receives the early and latter rain.**

This is speaking of the Spirit infilling, for no one is His without being Spiritfilled, and there was an early outpouring, and there will be a latter outpouring of His Spirit.

HOSEA 6:3

<u>Then shall we know, if we follow on to know Yahweh:</u> **His going forth is prepared as the morning; and he shall come unto us as the rain, as the latter and former rain unto the earth.**

Once again, speaking of the Spirit to those who follow Yahweh will end up receiving His Spirit.

ZECHARIAH 10:1

Ask ye of Yahweh for rain in the time of the latter rain; so **Yahweh shall make bright clouds and give them showers of rain, to every one grass in the field.**

We know he is speaking of the Spirit because rain comes from dark clouds, not bright clouds.

Job 29:21-23

Unto me men gave ear, and waited, and kept silence at my counsel. After my words they spake not again; and my speech dropped upon them. And **they waited for me as for the rain; and they opened their mouth wide as for the latter rain.**

In between the Former and the Latter Rain there is a dry period, and we are living in that dry period now since the days of Peter and Paul, and are now waiting for the Latter Rain to fall.

Acts 2:38 Then Peter said unto them, Repent, and be baptized every one of you in the name of Yahweh Messiah for the remission of transgressions, <u>and ye shall receive the gift of the Spirit.</u>

John 4:10 Immanuel answered and said unto her, **If thou knewest the gift of Yahweh, and who it is that saith to thee, Give me to drink**; **thou wouldest have asked of him, and he would have given thee living water.**

John 4:14 But whosoever drinketh of the water that I shall give him shall never thirst; but the water that I shall give him shall be in him a well of water springing up into everlasting life.

John 7:38 He that believeth on me, as the scripture hath said, out of his belly shall flow rivers of living water.

Revelation 21:6 And he said unto me, It is done. <u>I am Alpha and Omega, the beginning and the end.</u> **I will give unto him that is athirst of the fountain of the water of life freely.**

Revelation 22:17 And the Spirit and the bride say, Come. And let him that heareth say, **Come. And let him that is athirst come. And whosoever will, let him take the water of life freely.**

Revelation 6:9-11

9. And when he had opened the fifth seal, **I saw under the table the souls of them that were slain for the word of Yahweh, and for the testimony which they held:**

Notice: These believers were killed during the Fourth Seal of the Roman Empire for the testimony that they held.

10. And **they cried with a loud voice**, **saying, how long, O Yahweh, righteous and true, doest thou not judge and avenge our blood on them that dwell on the earth?**

11. <u>And white robes were given unto every one of them</u>: and **it was said unto them, that they should rest yet for a little season until their fellowservants also and their brethren, that should be murdered as they were, should be fulfilled.**

Notice: The space between those who are told to rest for a little season and the fellow brethren who are to be murdered as they were should be fulfilled. Why is this?

The Latter Rain will be poured out before Yahweh's return during the Tribulation Period, and <u>the last believers will be murdered for their testimony that Yahweh is true at this time.</u>

Joel 2: 27-32

27. And ye shall know that I am in the midst of Judaea, and that I am Yahweh your Almighty, and no one else: and my people shall never be ashamed.

28. And **it shall come to pass afterward, that I will pour out My Spirit upon all flesh; and your sons and your daughters shall prophesy, your old men shall dream dreams, your young men shall see visions:**

29. **And also, upon the servants and upon the handmaids in those days will I pour out My Spirit.**

30. And I will shew wonders in the heavens and in the earth, blood, and fire, and pillars of smoke.

31. The sun shall be turned into darkness, and the moon into blood, before the great and terrible day of Yahweh come.

32. **And it shall come to pass, that whosoever shall call on the name of Yahweh shall be delivered: for in Mount Zion and in Zion shall be deliverance, as Yahweh hath said, and in the remnant whom Yahweh shall call.**

Zechariah 12:10

10. And **I will pour out on the house of David and the inhabitants of Jerusalem a Spirit of praise and thanksgiving.** They will look on me, the one they have pierced, and they will mourn for him as one mourns for an only child, and grieve bitterly for him as one grieves for a firstborn son.

Acts 2:7

7. **And it shall come to pass in the last days, saith Yahweh, I will pour out of my Spirit upon all flesh: and your sons and your daughters shall prophesy, and your young men shall see visions, and your old men shall dream dreams:**

8. **And on my servants and on my handmaidens, I will pour out in those days of my Spirit; and they shall prophesy.**

CHAPTER 19

2 SETS OF GENTILES

GENTILES WERE AND WILL BE CALLED OUT FOR HIS NAMES SAKE. THE FIRST DURING THE FORMER RAIN, AND THE LAST WILL BE GENTILES CALLED OUT DURING THE LATTER RAIN FOR HIS NAME'S SAKE.

Just like there are two groups of 144,000, a former group (babies that were killed in place of Immanuel) and the latter group (those from the 12 tribes of Judaea that will call Yahweh back.)

Acts 15:14-18

14. **Simeon hath declared how Yahweh at the first did visit the Gentiles, to take out of them a people for his name.**

15. **And to this agree the words of the prophets; as it is written,**

16. After this I will return, and will build again the tabernacle of David, which is fallen down; and I will build again the ruins thereof, and I will set it up:

17. **That the residue of men might seek after Yahweh, and all the Gentiles, upon whom my name is called, saith Yahweh, who doeth all these things.**

18. Known unto Yahweh are all His works from the beginning of the world.

Isaiah 25:7

7: **And He will destroy in this mountain the face of the covering cast over all people and the vail that is spread over all nations.**

Jeremiah 16:19

19. **Yahweh, my strength, and my fortress, and my refuge in the day of affliction, <u>the Nations shall come unto thee from the ends of the earth, and shall say, surely our fathers have inherited lies, vanity, and things wherein there is no profit.</u>**

YAHWEH'S PEOPLE WILL BE IN THEIR HOMES LIKE THEY WERE IN THE DAYS OF PETER AND PAUL:

Yahweh's people will be in their homes, not in buildings or organizations.

1 Corinthians 1:11 For it hath been declared unto me of you, my brethren, by **THEM WHICH ARE OF THE HOUSE OF CHLOE**, that there are contentions among you.

Acts 8:3 But **Saul began to destroy the assembly. Going from house to house**, he dragged off men and women and put them in prison. [OBJ]

(We here see that each assembly Saul destroyed was found in a house.)

Romans 16:3-5 Greet **Priscilla and Aquila, my fellow-workers in Messiah Yahweh.** They risked their lives for me. Not only I **but all the assemblies of the Gentiles are grateful to them**. Greet also **the assemblies that meets at their house**.

1 Corinthians 16:19 The **assemblies in the province of Asia** send you greetings. **Aquila and Priscilla greet you warmly in Yahweh**, and **so does the assemblies that meets at their house.**

Colossians 4:15 Give my **greetings to the brothers at Laodicea,** and to **Nympha and the assembly that meets at her house.**

Philemon 1-2 Paul, a prisoner of Messiah Yahweh, and Timothy our brother. To Philemon our dear friend and fellowworker, to Apphia our sister, to **Archippus <u>our fellow-soldier and to the assembly that meets in your home.</u>**

Acts 5:42 And daily in the House of Yahweh, **and in every house**, **they ceased not to teach Yahweh Messiah.**

Now you know why the Messiah said what he said in the following verse.

Matthew 18:20

For where two or three are gathered together in MY NAME, there am I in the midst of them.

An assembly to Yahweh is where two or more people meet together in His Name. So whether it's two or a whole house full, that is an assembly. Say if the person in that house met with different people during different times of the day, each meeting would be considered an assembly, which could make one house assembly of Yahweh.

James 2:1-4 - My brothers, as believers in our esteemed Master, Yahweh Messiah, don't show favoritism. **Suppose a man comes into your meeting** wearing a gold ring and fine clothes, and a poor man in shabby clothes also comes in. If you show special attention to the man wearing fine clothes and say, "Here's a good seat for you," but say to the poor, "You stand there" or "Sit on the floor by my feet," have you not discriminated against yourselves and become judges with evil thoughts?

As you should see, they were in their homes.

THE BELIEVERS WHO WERE NOT FILLED WITH THE SPIRIT OF YAHWEH YET WERE BEING TAUGHT BY THE SPIRIT-FILLED BELIEVERS.

Ephesians 4:6,7,8; 11-16

6. One Yahweh and Father of all, who is above all, and through all, **and in you all**.

7. But unto every one of us is given the Spirit according to the measure of the gift of Yahweh.

8. Wherefore He saith, When He ascended up on high, He led captivity captive, and gave gifts unto men.

11.And He gave some, apostles [the original 12 disciples]; and some, prophets; [those who Yahweh spoke through] and some, evangelists [those who evangelize]; and some, shepherds [those who personally care for the sheep] and teachers [those who taught or gave instruction];

12.**For the perfecting of the believers**, **for the work of the ministry, for the edifying of the body of Yahweh:**

13.**Till we all come in the unity of the Faith**, **and of the knowledge of the Son of Yahweh**, unto **a perfect man, unto the measure of the stature of the fulness of Yahweh:**

14.**That we henceforth be no more children, tossed to and fro, and carried about with every wind of doctrine, by the sleight of men, and cunning craftiness, whereby they lie in wait to deceive;**

15.But speaking the truth in love, may grow up into Him in all things, which is the head, even Yahweh:

16.From whom the whole body fitly joined together and compacted by that which every joint supplieth, according to the effectual working in the measure of every part, maketh increase of the body unto the edifying of itself in love.

AS YOU SHOULD BE ABLE TO SEE AFTER READING ALL THIS, THAT PREACHERS OF TODAY ARE A LIE.

Mat 7:15 Beware of false prophets, which come to you in sheep's clothing, but inwardly they are ravening wolves.

Mat 7:16 Ye shall know them by their fruits. Do men gather grapes of thorns or figs of thistles?

Mat 7:17 Even so every good tree bringeth forth good fruit; but a corrupt tree bringeth forth evil fruit.

Mat 7:18 A good tree cannot bring forth evil fruit, neither can a corrupt tree bring forth good fruit.

Mat 7:19 Every tree that bringeth not forth good fruit is hewn down and cast into the fire.

Mat 7:20 Wherefore by their fruits ye shall know them.

Mat 7:21 Not everyone that saith unto me, Yahweh, Yahweh, shall enter into the kingdom of Yahweh; but he that doeth the will of my Father which is in heaven.

Mat 7:22 Many will say to me in that day, Yahweh, Yahweh, have we not prophesied in thy name and in thy name have cast out Satan? and in thy name done many wonderful works?

Mat 7:23 And then will I profess unto them, I never knew you: depart from me, ye that work iniquity. Mat 7:24 Therefore whosoever heareth these sayings of mine, and doeth them, I will liken him unto a wise man, which built his house upon a rock:

Mat 7:25 And the rain descended, and the floods came, and the winds blew, and beat upon that house; and it fell not; for it was founded upon a rock.

1 John 2:21, 27

21. <u>I have not written to you because you know not the truth,</u> but <u>because you know it,</u> and that **NO LIE IS OF THE TRUTH.**

27. But <u>**the annointing which ye have received of Him abideth in you**</u>, and <u>**ye need not that any man teach you**</u>: But as <u>**the same annointing teacheth you all things, and IS TRUTH, AND IS NO LIE, and even as it has taught you**</u>, <u>ye shall abide in Him</u>.

CHAPTER 20

SPIRITUALISM AND CHRISTIANITY

These are an abomination unto Yahweh:

1. Aeromancy: Air.

2. Aleuromany: Flour.

3. Arithmancy (Numerology) - Number; each letter has a number value, as in a name.

4. Astrology: The study professing to foretell the future and interpret the influence of the heavenly bodies upon the destinies of men.

5. Bibliomancy: Book, usually the Bible.

6. Charm: Something worn to ward off evil or ensure good luck.

7. Charmer: To influence by or as if by a spell; bewitch.

8. Crysallomancy: Crystal gazing.

9. Divination: The act or art of knowing the future of that which is hidden or unknown.

10. Enchant: To put a spell upon; bewitch.

11. Fortuneteller: One who claims to foretell events in a person's future.

12. Graphology: Handwriting.

13. Horoscope: Zodiacal signs by which astrologers profess to tell a person's future.

14. Kypomancy: Tea leaves in a cup.

15. Medium: One through whom the spirits of the dead are believed to communicate with the living. Black magic or sorcery.

16. Necromancy: The art of divining the future through alleged communication with the dead. Black magic or sorcery.

17. Oneiromancy: Dreams.

18. Ouija: A device consisting of a large board inscribed with the alphabet and other characters and over which moves a small rectangular board resting on three legs, the pointer of which is thought to spell out mediumistic communications.

19. Palmistry: The art or practice of supposedly discovering a person's past or future from the lines and marks in the palm of the hand.

20. Rhabdomancy: Rods, such as a divining rod indicating presence of water, minerals, or oil.

21. Sorcerer: A wizard; conjurer; magician.

22. Sorcery: Alleged employment of spiritual agencies; witchcraft.

23. Spiritualism: The belief that the spirits of the dead communicate with and manifest their presence to the living.

24. Tarot: One of a set of playing cards with grilled or checkered backs employed by fortunetellers and gypsies in foretelling future events.

25. Witch: A woman who practices sorcery.

26. Witchcraft: The practice of powers of witches or wizards.

27. Wizard : A male witch; sorcerer; enchanter.

THERE ARE MANY MORE ALSO. THESE ARE JUST A FEW.

What does the word of Yahweh say about all this?

Deuteronomy 4:19 And lest thou lift up thine eyes unto heaven, and when thou seest the sun, and the moon, and the stars, even all the host of heaven, shouldest be driven to worship them, and serve them, which Yahweh hath divided unto all nations under the whole heaven.

Deuteronomy 7:3 Neither shalt thou make marriages with them; thy daughter thou shalt not give unto his son, nor his daughter shalt thou take unto thy son.

Exodus 22:18 Thou shalt not suffer a witch to live.

Daniel 2:27 Daniel answered in the presence of the king, and said, the secret which the king hath demanded cannot the wise [men], the astrologers, the magicians, the soothsayers, shew unto the king;

Leviticus 19:31 Regard not them that have familiar spirits, neither seek after wizards, to be defiled by them: I am Yahweh.

Deuteronomy 13:1-3

1. If there arise among you a prophet, or a dreamer of dreams, and giveth thee a sign or a wonder,

2. And the sign or the wonder come to pass, whereof he spake unto thee, saying, let us go after other deities, which thou hast not known, and let us serve them;

3 Thou shalt not hearken unto the words of that prophet, or that dreamer of dreams: for Yahweh proveth you, to know whether ye love Yahweh with all your heart and with all your soul.

Micah 3:7 Then shall the seers be ashamed, and the diviners confounded: yea, they shall all cover their lips; for there is no answer of Yahweh

Deuteronomy 18:10-12

¹⁰ There shall not be found among you anyone that maketh his son or his daughter to pass through the fire, or that useth divination, or an observer of times, or an enchanter, or a witch.

¹¹ Or a charmer, or a consulter with familiar spirits, or a wizard, or a necromancer.

¹² For all that do these things are an abomination unto Yahweh: and because of these abominations Yahweh doth drive them out from before thee.

Zachariah 10:2 ² For the idols have spoken vanity, and the diviners have seen a lie, and have told false dreams; they comfort in vain: therefore, they went their way as a flock, they were troubled, because there was no shepherd.

Micah 5:12 ¹² And I will cut off witchcrafts out of thine hand; and thou shalt have no more soothsayers:

Isaiah 8:19-20

¹⁹ And when they shall say unto you, seek unto them that have familiar spirits, and unto wizards that peep, and that mutter: should not a people seek unto their deity? for the living to the dead?

²⁰ To the law and to the testimony: if they speak not according to this word, it is because there is no light in them.

Jeremiah 27:9-10

⁹ Therefore hearken not ye to your prophets, nor to your diviners, nor to your dreamers, nor to your enchanters, nor to your sorcerers, which speak unto you, saying, Ye shall not serve the king of Babylon:

¹⁰ **For they prophesy a lie unto you, to remove you far from your land; and that I should drive you out, and ye should perish.**

Leviticus 20:27 A man also or woman that hath a familiar spirit, or that is a wizard, shall surely be put to death: they shall stone them with stones: their blood shall be upon them.

Malachi 3:5 And I will come near to you to judgment; and I will be a swift witness against the sorcerers, and against the adulterers, and against false swearers, and against those that oppress the hireling in his wages, the widow, and the fatherless, and that turn aside the stranger from his right, and fear not me, saith Yahweh of hosts.

Galatians 5:19-21

¹⁹ **Now the works of the flesh are manifest, which are these; Adultery, fornication, uncleanness, lasciviousness,**

²⁰ **Idolatry, witchcraft, hatred, variance, emulations, wrath, strife, seditions, heresies,**

²¹ **Envying's, murders, drunkenness, reveling, and such like: of the which I tell you before, as I have also told you in time past, that they which do such things shall not inherit the kingdom of Yahweh.**

Revelation 21:8 But the fearful, and unbelieving, and the abominable, and murderers, and whoremongers, and sorcerers, and idolaters, and all liars, shall have their part in the lake which burneth with fire and brimstone: which is the second death.

1 Timothy 4:1 Now the Spirit speaketh expressly, that in the latter times some shall depart from the faith, giving heed to seducing spirits, and doctrines of devils;

1 John 4:1 Beloved, believe not every spirit, but try the spirits whether they are of Yahweh: because many false prophets are gone out into the world.

Jesus - sun deity

Amen - sun deity

God - sun and moon deity

Lord - sun deity

"WHEN YOU USE LORD AND GOD YOU PROMOTE UNIVERSALISM"

Adonai - sun deity

Christ - sun deity

Sin - moon deity

Allah - moon deity

The above are just a few of the SUN and MOON deities that Christians serve under.

"A LITTLE RAT POISON WITH THE GOOD STUFF STILL KILLS THE RAT!

CHAPTER 21

THE TIMELINE:

WW3 >>>> 7 Year Peace Plan >>>> Moses and Eliyah bring back the truth Truth taught to every person on earth - Yahweh's Spirit poured out >>>>> Moses and Eliyah killed midway of Peace Plan >>>> Pope takes power >>>> NO 3rd House of Yahweh, Dome of the Rock will be used >>>> Start of Tribulation Period >>>> Christianity made World Religion - Mark of the Beast given (CROSS) - Yahweh's elect persecuted and killed >>>> Armageddon >> Satan will make himself known and will help the world armies fight Yahweh and his Messengers before Yahweh's return>> Return of Yahweh >>>> Millennial Kingdom on earth >>>> Satan raised from grave to deceive the world one last time >>>> White Throne Judgement >>>> End of this world, it burns up with all the wicked with it >>>> New Heaven and Earth >>>> Yahweh lives on the New Earth with His Elect.

SALVATION COMES AGAIN DURING THE 7YEAR PEACE PLAN AFTER WW3:

THE LAST DAY TRUTH WILL BE TAUGHT TO ALL THE WORLD INHABITANTS AGAIN, IN YAHWEH'S NAME, AND THE LATTER RAIN OF YAHWEH'S SPIRIT POURED OUT AT THIS TIME, DURING THE 7 YEAR PEACE PLAN:

Revelation 14:6-7

6. And I saw another Messenger fly, in the midst of heaven, having the "Everlasting Word...to teach unto them that dwell on the earth, and to every nation,

7. Saying with a loud voice, Fear Yahweh, and give praise to Him; for the hour of His judgment is come: and worship him that made heaven, and earth, and the sea, and the fountains of waters.

Revelation 11:3 And I will give *power* unto my two witnesses, and they shall prophesy a thousand two hundred *and* threescore days, clothed in sackcloth.

NOTE: 3 ½ years the first 3 ½ years of the 7-Year Peace Plan. The last 3 ½ years is the Tribulation Period.

Malachi 4:5-6

5 Behold, I will send you Elijah the prophet before the coming of the great and dreadful day of Yahweh:

6 And he shall turn the heart of the fathers to the children, and the heart of the children to their fathers, lest I come and smite the earth with a curse.

Luke 1:17 And he shall go before him in the spirit and power of Eliyah, to turn the hearts of the fathers to the children, and the disobedient to the wisdom of the just; to make ready a people prepared for Yahweh.

Matthew 24:14 And this Word of the Kingdom shall be taught in all the world for a witness unto all nations and then shall the end come.

These are the future 7-Year Peace Plan believers, and the book of Acts will be re-lived at that time. They will receive the Latter Rain of Yahweh's Spirit when the truth is taught to every person on earth at that time. This has been Satan's world before that time comes all the way back to the 11 persecutions of the Roman Empire that killed off all the elect back then.

Ephesians 4:6,7,8; 11-16

6. One Yahweh and Father of all, who is above all, and through all, <u>and in you all</u>.

7. But unto every one of us is given the Spirit according to the measure of the gift of Yahweh.

8. Wherefore He saith, When He ascended up on high, He led captivity captive and gave gifts unto men.

11. And He gave some, apostles [the original 12 disciples]; and some, prophets; [those who Yahweh spoke through] and some, evangelists [those who evangelize]; and some, shepherds [those who personally care for the sheep] and teachers [those who taught or gave instruction];

12. <u>For the perfecting of the believers</u>, <u>for the work of the ministry, for the edifying of the body of Yahweh:</u>

13. <u>Till we all come in the unity of the Faith</u>, <u>and of the knowledge of the Son of Yahweh</u>, unto <u>a perfect man, unto the measure of the stature of the fulness of Yahweh:</u>

14. <u>That we henceforth be no more children, tossed to and fro, and carried about with every wind of doctrine, by the sleight of men, and cunning craftiness, whereby they lie in wait to deceive;</u>

15. But speaking the truth in love, may grow up into Him in all things, which is the head, even Yahweh:

16. From whom the whole body fitly joined together and compacted by that which every joint supplieth, according to the effectual working in the measure of every part, maketh increase of the body unto the edifying of itself in love.

<u>In other words, when you first believe, you become a believer, but you are not Spirit-filled yet. So, the Spirit-filled believers were the ones who taught the new</u>

believers in Yahweh Messiah until Yahweh has seen fit to fill them with His Spirit. The Spirit-filled people were taught by the Spirit and knew all things. The believers who were not Spirit-filled had to be taught of Yahweh's ways.

Salvation is when you are filled with Yahweh's Spirit and not before.

They did not have salvation when they asked for forgiveness or when they were baptized in His Name, Yahweh. So, they were not so-called saved at that time.

Let me explain what the scriptures really teach: At the time of repentance, asking for forgiveness of transgressions is the first step to salvation. The person became an Apprentice for the infilling of Yahweh's Spirit, and Yahweh started helping them clean themselves up; at baptism, this was the second step to salvation, and they became a Candidate for the infilling of Yahweh's Spirit. This is when the person was thriving to serve Yahweh and Yahweh is still helping them to clean themselves up, so His Spirit can dwell in them. When this was done, they became a Journeyman, which was the third and last step to believing, and that is when the Master Yahweh filled the people with His Spirit, and this was a true believer in Yahweh.

Acts 5:32 And we are His witnesses of these things; and so is also the Spirit, whom Yahweh hath given to them that obey Him.

John 7:39 (*But this spake he of the Spirit, which they that believed on him should receive* for the Spirit was not yet given; because Immanuel was not yet esteemed.

Acts 1:8 But ye shall receive power, after that the Spirit comes upon you: and ye shall be witnesses unto me both in Zion, and in all Judaea, and in Samaria, and unto the uttermost part of the earth.

Hosea 6:3 Then shall we know, if we follow on to know Yahweh: his going forth is prepared as the morning; and he shall come unto us as the rain, as the latter and former rain unto the earth.

Those from Pentecost to the last of the 10 Roman Emperor Persecutions received the Former Rain of Yahweh's Spirit infilling. The future 7-Year Peace Plan elect will receive the Latter Rain of Yahweh's Spirit infilling.

Hebrews 2:3,4

3. How shall we escape, if we neglect so great salvation; which at the first began to be spoken by the Master and was confirmed unto us by them that heard him.

4. Yahweh also bearing them witness, both with signs and wonders, and with diver's miracles, and gifts of the Spirit, according to His own will?

Luke 10:19 Behold, I give unto you power to tread on serpents and scorpions, and over all the power of the enemy: and nothing shall by any means hurt you.

NOTE: As you should be able to see, Christians do not have Yahweh's Spirit, nor do the so-called Pentecostals; as a matter of fact, no one today has Yahweh's Spirit infilling.

Romans 8:9 But ye are not in the flesh but in the Spirit, if so be the Spirit of Yahweh dwells in you. Now if any man has not the Spirit of Yahweh, he is none of His.

2 Corinthians 13:5 Examine yourselves, whether ye be in the faith; prove your own selves. Know ye not your own selves, how that Yahweh Messiah is in you, except ye be reprobates?

Now watch: If you are alive during the 7-Year Peace Plan, you will hear the whole truth and can believe it or not. This will lead to tribulation of the persecutions and killings of the elect. That is another reason you MUST have Yahweh's Spirit infilling for salvation, too.

How about us today? If you die before the 7-Year Peace Treaty, Yahweh will raise you up during the Millennial Kingdom and teach you Himself, but there will be no salvation at that time for those who are taught by Him. WHY? Because there will be no more excuses for when Satan is raised from the grave, which Yahweh will have killed at His coming. Satan will be given one last chance to deceive the world. Those people lived in Satan's world and then lived in Yahweh's Kingdom taught by Yahweh Himself, so they must be tried like in the days of Peter and Paul, and the coming Tribulation Period of the elect as they were tried and tested will also be tried and tested. So, they have a choice to believe in Yahweh, which is life, or Satan, which is death. This is the final battle of judgment.

Daniel 7:25 And he shall speak great words against Yahweh, and shall wear out the Elect of Yahweh, and think to change times and laws: and they shall be given into his hand until a time and times and the dividing of time.

The Elect during the last 3 ½ year Tribulation Period and the last 3 ½ years of the 7-Year Peace Plan will be given into the Pope's hand at this time.

The following chapter of Daniel 12 speaks about the time of the 7-Year Peace Plan and the Tribulation Period just before Yahweh returns.

Matthew 24:29-31 – <u>A POST TRIBULATION "CATCHING UP"</u>

[29] **<u>Immediately after the tribulation of those days</u>** shall the sun be darkened, and the moon shall not give her light, and the stars shall fall from heaven, and the powers of the heavens shall be shaken:

³⁰ And **then shall appear the sign of the Son of man in heaven:** and then shall all the tribes of the earth mourn, and they shall see the Son of man coming in the clouds of heaven with power and great glory.

³¹ And **he shall send his Messengers with a great sound of a trumpet, and they shall gather together his elect from the four winds, from one end of heaven to the other.**

Daniel 12:1-13

1 And at that time shall Michael stand up, the great prince which standeth for the children of thy people: and there shall be a time of trouble, such as never was since there was a nation even to that same time: and at that time thy people shall be delivered, every one that shall be found written in the book.

2 And many of them that sleep in the dust of the earth shall awake, some to everlasting life, and some to shame and everlasting contempt.

3 And they that be wise shall shine as the brightness of the firmament; and they that turn many to righteousness as the stars for ever and ever.

4 But thou, O Daniel, shut up the words, and seal the book, even to the time of the end: many shall run to and fro, and knowledge shall be increased.

5 Then I Daniel looked, and, behold, there stood other two, the one on this side of the bank of the river, and the other on that side of the bank of the river.

6 And one said to the man clothed in linen, which was upon the waters of the river, how long shall it be to the end of these wonders?

7 And I heard the man clothed in linen, which was upon the waters of the river, when he held up his right hand and his left hand unto heaven, and sware by him that liveth forever that it shall be for a time, times, and a half; and when he shall have accomplished to scatter the power of the righteous people, all these things shall be finished.

8 And I heard, but I understood not: then said I, O my Master, what shall be the end of these things?

9 And he said, go thy way, Daniel: for the words are closed and sealed till the time of the end.

10 Many shall be purified, and made white, and tried; but the wicked shall do wickedly: and none of the wicked shall understand; but the wise shall understand.

11 And from the time that the daily offering shall be taken away, and the abomination that maketh desolate set up, there shall be a thousand two hundred and ninety days.

12 Blessed is he that waiteth, and cometh to the thousand three hundred and five and thirty days.

13 But go thou thy way till the end be: for thou shalt rest and stand in thy lot at the end of the days.

CHAPTER 22

THOSE TAUGHT BY YAHWEH

It does not matter if a person is a homosexual, committed suicide, murdered someone, died from a drug overdose, a prostitute, aborted a baby or babies, or is in prison for wrongdoings. We live in Satan's world, and his society has caused all these things, and Yahweh is going to give man one last opportunity to clean themselves up and be forgiven. Just accept the truth when it comes. The ONLY THING that is not forgivable is once a person is filled with Yahweh's Spirit and after tasting of the good things then the person turns their back on Yahweh and walks away, they re-kill the Messiah, and there will be no more forgiveness for that person only judgment in the Lake of Fire, that is blasphemy of the Spirit.

The Millennial Kingdom is so Yahweh can teach those who never heard the truth from those after the 11 Roman persecutions up to the 7-Year Peace Plan. Yahweh could end it all when He returns, the Millennial Kingdom is to show His mercy upon all the people to give them all a chance for salvation, though few will accept it from their brainwashing.

This is Satan's world now, and has no salvation. Now, how is Yahweh, with His mercy, going to work it out for all people to hear the truth and to believe it or not because he cannot judge a person who has never heard the whole truth or given the opportunity for salvation.

Now watch: If you are alive during the 7-Year Peace Plan, you will hear the whole truth and have the opportunity to believe it or not at that time. This will lead to tribulation of the elect and persecution. That is another reason why you MUST have Yahweh's Spirit infilling for salvation.

How about us today? If you die before the 7-Year Peace Treaty, Yahweh will raise you up during the Millennial Kingdom and teach you Himself, but there will be no salvation at that time for those who are taught by Him. WHY?

Because there will be no more excuses for when Satan is raised from the grave, which Yahweh killed at His coming. Satan will be given one last chance to deceive the world. Those people lived in Satan's world and then lived in Yahweh's Kingdom taught by Yahweh Himself, so they must be tried like in the days of Peter and Paul, and the coming Tribulation Period of the elect as they were tried and tested will also be tried and tested.

Romans 10:14 How then shall they call on him in whom they have not believed? and **HOW SHALL THEY BELIEVE IN HIM OF WHOM THEY HAVE NOT HEARD? and how shall they hear without a teacher?**

Acts 24:15 And have hope toward Yahweh, which they themselves also allow, that there shall be a resurrection of the dead, both of the just and unjust.

Daniel 7:12 As concerning the rest of the beasts, they had their dominion taken away: yet their lives were prolonged for a season and time.

Now, why would the rest of the nation's lives be prolonged? The people that were left on earth after Yahweh collected His elect were killed and burned up. So, the earth was void of life until Yahweh came right back to this earth with the elect with Him. In 2 Timothy 2:12, it says, if we suffer, we shall also reign with him: if we deny him, he also will deny us. What people will the elect reign over each other? No. They will reign over those Yahweh raises who never heard the truth.

Daniel 12:1-2

1. And at that time shall Michael stand up, the great King which standeth for the children of thy people: and there shall be a time of trouble, such as never

was since there was a nation even to that same time: and at that time thy people shall be delivered, every one that shall be found written in the book.

NOTICE: In verse one, it says only those who are found in the book [Book of Life] shall be delivered. So that is the dead and living who lived and suffered persecution and death.

2. And many of them that sleep in the dust of the earth shall awake, some to everlasting life, and some to shame and everlasting contempt.

In verse 2, this is another group raised from the dead, which are those who never heard the truth. They are taught by Yahweh, and some will believe, and others will not when Satan is loosed, so they awake without knowledge, and their end is whether they believed Yahweh's teachings or not. These are those who were not found in the Book of Life because they never heard the whole truth. These are those from the nations that the Elect will rule over with Yahweh during the Millennium.

Jeremiah 16:19 "O Yahweh, my strength, and my fortress, and my refuge in the day of affliction, the Gentiles shall come unto thee from the ends of the earth, and shall say, surely our fathers have inherited lies, vanity, and *things* wherein *there is* no profit."

This cannot happen at the White Throne Judgement; it happens during the Millennial Kingdom, and these people who were raised never heard the truth. Everyone must hear and know the truth before they can be judged.

Jeremiah 3:17 At that time they will call Zion the throne of Yahweh and all nations will gather in Zion to honor the name of Yahweh. No longer will they follow the stubbornness of their evil hearts.

Revelation 22:14-15

14. Blessed are they that do his commandments, that they may have right to the tree of life and may enter in through the gates into the city.

15. For without are dogs, and sorcerers, and whoremongers, and murderers, and idolaters, and whosoever loveth and maketh a lie.

Here again, how can there be any non-believers outside the city gates if Yahweh did not raise them up for the Millennial Kingdom to be taught the truth?

Isaiah 2:3 And many people shall go and say, come ye, and let us go up to the mountain of Yahweh, to the House of Yahweh of Jacob; and He will teach us of His ways, and we will walk in his paths: for out of Zion shall go forth the law, and the Word of Yahweh from Zion.

Why would they need to be taught His ways if they were not believers at that time? The elect was filled with Yahweh's Spirit and know all things.

Isaiah 54:13 All your children shall be taught by Yahweh, and great shall be the peace of your children.

Here again, why are they taught by Yahweh? They never heard the truth.

John 6:45 It is written in the Prophets: "They will all be taught by Yahweh 'Everyone who has heard the Father and learned from Him comes to Me."

Hebrews 8:11 No longer will they teach their neighbor, or say to one another, 'Know Yahweh,' because they will all know Me, from the least of them to the greatest.

NOTE: As you should be able to see, the Word of Yahweh was HID. Look how many generations of people who never heard the truth and had the choice to believe or not to believe. It is THESE PEOPLE that Yahweh will teach during the Millennium, so there will be no excuses when Yahweh releases Satan from the grave one last time, then the final Judgment on this world and its people.

You must also remember that Yahweh killed and burned up every person left on earth after He collected His Elect. So, the earth had no people alive on it. So, these were resurrected who never heard the truth of Yahweh and the opportunity to believe it or not.

YAHWEH'S SPACECRAFT

Yahweh returns in spacecraft, and all the

wheat will be caught up in them, The ones

that are saved from Yahweh's wrath, those

who had served Him.

Then Yahweh and His Messengers, like birds

flying, burns up all the chaff. People never

dreamed that all this will be done with Yahweh's

spacecraft.

After this, a great voice of many people in heaven and praising Yahweh, for

avenging the blood of His elect, while the smoke ascended their way.

They are in spacecraft in heaven above the earth when this praise is done.

Then the elect come right back to this earth with Yahweh Messiah, the Son.

During His Kingdom, Yahweh teaches all those who never heard His Word,

Between Paul's time and the 7 Year Peace Plan whose minds were blurred.

Who died in Satan's world from our non-believing ancestor's pagan lies,

Those who did not believe and turned the truth of Yahweh under a guise.

The whole truth will be taught during the 7-Year Peace Plan; be ready for it.

The miracles and healings once again, just like in the Acts, so do not quit.

Want a spaceship ride, then Yahweh is the Messiah for those who survive?

From that day forward, you will never have to die, forever and eternal alive!

By Gary Wendell Stanfield

PERMISSION GIVEN TO USE FROM J. FRANCIS, WHO HOLDS THE COPYRIGHT.

THE "CATCHING UP"

New Heaven and Earth.

¹ Now I saw a new heaven and a new earth, for the first heaven and the first earth had passed away. Also, there was no more sea.

² Then I, John, saw the righteous city, New Zion, coming down out of heaven from Yahweh, prepared as a bride adorned for her husband.

³ And I heard a loud voice from heaven saying, "Behold, the tabernacle of Yahweh *is* with men, and He will dwell with them, and they shall be His people. Yahweh Himself will be with them *and be* their Mighty One.

⁴ And Yahweh will wipe away every tear from their eyes; there shall be no more death, nor sorrow, nor crying. There shall be no more pain, for the former things have passed away."

CHAPTER 23

THE DOME OF THE ROCK:

HISTORY FIRST: The Roman Zion

Encyclopedia Britannica Aelia Capitolina city founded in AD 135 by the Romans on the ruins of Zion, which their forces, under Titus, had destroyed in 70 C.E. The name was given after the Second Jewish Revolt (132–135) in honor of the emperor Hadrian (whose nomen, or clan name, was Aelius) as well as the deities of the Capitoline Triad (Jupiter, Juno, and Minerva). A sanctuary to Jupiter was built on the TEMPLE MOUNT, and statues of Roman deities were erected in the city in intentional violation of Old Covenant law. The area was walled, and a large foreign population was imported; Jews were generally forbidden entrance to the city. The present walls of the Old City of Zion follow the layout of the Roman walls. The name was used until Christianity became the official religion of the Roman Empire in the 4th century. A temple to Jupiter was constructed on the Temple Mount, and idols of Roman deities were erected throughout the city in a deliberate and malicious violation of Yahweh's law.

NOTE: In the above encyclopedia article, where the House of Yahweh was, it's called the Temple Mount, which came from the Gentiles calling it that. Jews did not have temples. The House of Yahweh was on Mount Moriah, below the Roman Fort.

The Wailing Wall is the footing wall of the old Roman Fort. Just more lies for people to be deceived by.

Daniel 11:45 And he shall plant <u>the temple of his palace </u>between the seas in the righteous mountain; yet he shall come to his end, and none shall help him.

ORDER OUT OF CHAOS

There are a few in this world,

Their control of people is hurled.

Aggressively pushing agendas and knowing what that does.

The evil of power and greed,

Is on what these people feed.

Taking away every freedom

To make a one world kingdom.

Order through chaos is the theme,

All for to hear the people scream.

Knowing that is all people will do,

While evil is tightening the screw.

This is now the age of delusion,

People believing in evolution.

Brainwashed and put to sleep,

No clue to what they will reap.

This world will worship a man,

It's all in the prophetic plan.

One that wears religious garb,

To the Papacy this is a barb.

So wake-up world it's coming,

The final scenes are drumming.

The Tribulation Period is at hand,

Will you be one who will withstand?

By Gary Wendell Stanfield

YOU SHALL SEE

In time, the entire world shall see,

A One World Government, there shall be.

Ruled by no one else, but the Papacy.

Proven by history and by prophecy.

The Pope cannot wait to take his throne,

When in Zion he shall be shown. That's

when people will moan and groan, When

this deceitful truth is finally sown.

Then the entire world shall see,

What the Mark of the Beast will be.

Many will think it will set them free,

but this will start the killing spree.

By Gary Wendell Stanfield

The building is not that of a typical mosque.

The Dome of the Rock Façade and what it is hiding, the Temple of God that the Pope will move his throne to.

Cross section of the Dome (print from 1887, after the first detailed drawings of the Dome, made by

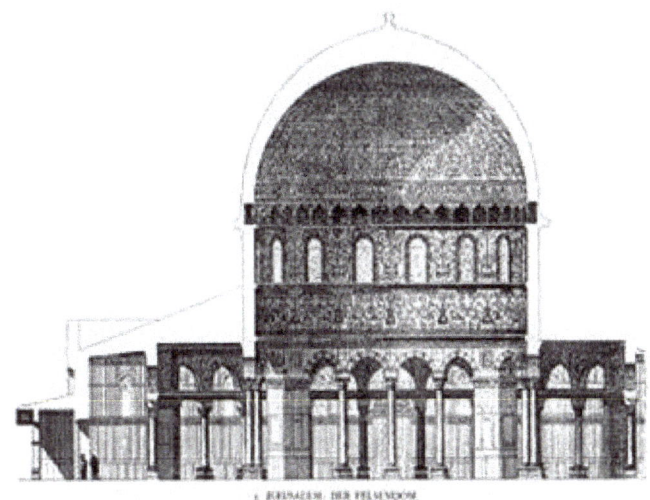

Frederick Catherwood in 1833).

The Mausoleum of Theodoric Ravenna in Italy and the Imperial Mausoleum of Romulus Augustus in Italy are octagons and look like the Dome of the Rock.

Something interesting: OCTOBER- From the Latin word "octo," meaning eight, which was the eighth month of the calendar. (Yet we use it as the tenth month?) It was built by the Romans and not the Muslims, by its octagonal shape with the dome. History has been changed and twisted to deceive mankind. The Pope will move his throne to the Dome of the Rock, which is the name people are used to it being called, but it was first named the Temple of God.

The Dome of the Rock is Roman architecture, not Muslim. The octagonal plan of the structure may also have been influenced by the Byzantine Church of the Seat of Mary. Plus, the Dome is just like the one at Saint Peter's in Rome.

The Church of Nativity was first built by Constantine in 326 C.E. It had an octagonal floor, just like the shape of the Dome of the Rock. Justinian destroyed it and built a larger one in its place, the one that is seen today.

It was Constantine who had the original octagon building built as a temple since the marble and mosaic parts of the dome were added centuries after it was built. Just like the Church of Nativity was originally an octagon shaped building built by Constantine. In the next paragraph below under this one, you will see where the Christians renamed the Dome of the Rock the "Temple of God" and made it a church. What did Constantine name the scriptures after he redid them and made them void of salvation? *Constantine then decreed that the New Testimonies would thereafter be called the word of the Roman Savior God (Life of Constantine, vol. iii, p. 29) [OR the Word of God.] It was Constantine and his mother who had churches built over what they thought were the religious sites in Jerusalem.* In 326-28, Helena undertook a trip to the Holy Places in Palestine. According to Eusebius of Caesarea, she was responsible for the construction or beautification of two churches, the Church of the Nativity, Bethlehem, and the Church of Eleona on the Mount of Olives, sites of Christ's birth and ascension, respectively. Local founding legend attributes to Helena's orders the construction of a church in Egypt to identify the Burning Bush of Sinai. *The Messiah was killed on a real live Olive Tree, not a Cross. They used a rope around the wrists to hang him from the tree, not 3 nails*

It is said that she (Constantine's mother) also found the Cross and 3 nails, so Constantine had the Church of the Holy Sepulcher *built over the site. Lies and deceit.*

A.C. Cresswell, in his book *Origin of the Plan of the Dome of the Rock,* notes that those who built the shrine used the measurements of the Church of the Holy Sepulchre. [Picture below:]

Surviving descriptions of Christian pilgrimages to the Holy Land and Jerusalem date from the 4th century. The *Itinerarium Burdigalense* ("Bordeaux Itinerary"), the oldest surviving Christian *itinerarium*, was written by the anonymous "Pilgrim of Bordeaux" recounting the stages of a pilgrimage to Jerusalem in the years 333 and 334. General context of early Christian pilgrimage is provided by E.D. Hunt, *Holy Land Pilgrimage in the Late Roman Empire AD 312-460* 1982.

<u>Pilgrimage was encouraged by church fathers like Saint Jerome and established by Helena</u>, the mother of Constantine the Great.

Church of the Holy Sepulchre. St. Helen and St. Macarius, Patriarch of Jerusalem, had identified with the burial site of Jesus. The surrounding rock was cut away, and the Tomb was encased in a structure called the *Edicule* (from the Latin *aediculum*, a small building) in the center of the rotunda. The dome of the rotunda was completed by the end of the 4th century.

In 1099, the Crusaders called the Temple Mount "Templum Domini" and turned the Dome of the Rock into a church, adding a cross on the dome. When Christianity won back Jerusalem/Zion, they did not destroy the Dome of the Rock; they renamed it the "Temple of God" (Which was the original name given to it, to begin with, when it was built by Constantine), so the above verse is literally true with the temple of God.

That's why it is not the House of Yahweh that the Pope will sit in. There will be no 3rd House of Yahweh until Yahweh builds it during the Millennial Kingdom. Jews did not use temples or synagogues. The pagans did. Jews used the House of Yahweh. You can only ask yourself, did all this happen to take people's eyes off Rome and to look at the Muslims as the creators of the Dome of the Rock? I believe that is exactly what happened. Everything must do with pagan Rome in the last days, nothing about Islam, which was started by the Papacy.

The actual temple is inside the walls that were built later to surround the actual temple. It was at this time that the Mount was called the Temple Mount. This is not the site where the House of Yahweh was. There won't be another House of Yahweh until Yahweh rebuilds it during the Millennial Kingdom.

Seems the church that was built over the cave where the Messiah was supposed to have been born is a lie, too. The Dome of the Rock is actually built on part of the old Roman Fort. No one really knew where the House of Yahweh was located since it was destroyed in 70 C.E. They ran the Jews off with the threat of death if they ever stepped foot back there.

Aelia Capitolina was a Roman colony founded during Emperor **Hadrian's visit to Judaea** in 129/130 AD, [1][2] centered around Jerusalem, which had been almost totally razed after the siege of 70 C.E.

The foundation of Aelia Capitolina and the construction of a temple to Jupiter at the site of the former temple. **Constantine had this temple torn down and built the Temple of God in its place.**

"Among Muslims of Islam's earliest era, it was referred to as Madinat bayt al-Maqdis ("City of the Temple"), which was restricted to the Temple Mount."

Official seals of the Order's Grand Masters (such as Everard des Barres and Renaud de Vichiers), Seal below you can see that the interior of the Dome of the Rock is the original "Temple of God" without the outer walls and why it looks like it does today.

The Dome of the Rock is Roman architecture. The Templum Domini, as they called the Dome of the Rock. As you should be able to see, this was hundreds of years after Constantine built the "Temple of God."

I want to show you something else that is very interesting to prove the above.

Revelation 11:1

1. And there was given me a reed like unto a rod: and the Messenger stood, saying, Rise, and measure the temple of God, and the altar, and them that worship therein. [Remember this is the temple of Constantine]

NOTE: Verse 1 is speaking of the so-called Temple of God, which is the Dome of the Rock being spoken of here. The altar being a ROCK that Abraham was going to offer Isaac is not true. His was made out of wood, according to the scriptures.

Let's talk about that rock.

Inside Saint John's Baptistery a religious building in Florence, Italy.

The Dome of the Rock is Roman architecture. Constantine had this built.

Let's talk about that rock.

There is no mention of a ROCK when Abraham was going to offer Isaac in Genesis chapter 22.

Genesis 22:9 And they came to the place which Yahweh had told him of; and **ABRAHAM BUILT AN ALTAR THERE** and **LAID THE WOOD IN ORDER**, and bound Isaac his son, and **LAID HIM ON THE ALTAR UPON THE WOOD.**

Absolutely not one huge rock. Abraham built the altar himself.

One more thing, it was Constantine and his mother who built these Christian churches on top of religious sites that his mother had found, none are the actual scriptural sites. Some had bigger churches built on the sites, tearing down the ones Constantine had built? The House of Yahweh was destroyed in 70 C.E.

CHAPTER 24

LAZARUS AND THE RICH MAN

Matthew 13:13-17,34

13   Therefore speak I to them in parables: because they are seeing, see not: and hearing, they hear not, neither do they understand.

14   And in them is fulfilled the prophecy of Isaiah, which saith, by hearing ye shall hear, and shall not understand: and seeing ye shall see, and shall not perceive.

15   For this people's heart is waxed gross, and their ears are dull of hearing, and their eyes they have closed, lest at any time they should see with their eyes, and hear with their ears, and should understand with their heart, and should be converted, and I should heal them.

16   But blessed are your eyes, for they see: and your ears, for they hear.

17   For verily I say unto you, that many Prophets, and righteous men have desired to see those things which ye see, and have not seen them: and to hear those things which ye hear, and have not heard them.

34 That it might be fulfilled which was spoken by the prophet, saying, I will open my mouth in parables; I will utter things which have been kept secret from the foundation of the world.

Let me first set the stage for Lazarus and the rich man, go back a few verses before the start of this parable.

Notice: Immanuel is talking to the Pharisees just before he begins the parable on Lazarus and the rich man because they sneered at him about the last parable he had spoken about.

Luke 16:14-16

14: And the Pharisees also, who were covetous, heard all these things: and they derided him.

15: And he said unto them, Ye are they which justify yourselves before men; but Yahweh knoweth your hearts: for that which is highly esteemed among men is abomination in the sight of Yahweh.

16: The law and the prophets were until John: since that time the kingdom of Yahweh is taught, and every man presseth into it.

Now, let's go to the parable. We will take one or two verses at a time to explain each verse as we go:

Luke 16:19 There was a certain rich man, which was clothed in purple and fine linens, and fared sumptuously every day:

The rich man being the Pharisee. In this next verse, Immanuel is talking about how high the Scribes and Pharisees live.

Matthew 23:4-7

4: For they bind heavy burdens and grievous to be borne, and lay them on men's shoulders; but they themselves will not move them with one of their fingers.

5: But all their works they do for to be seen of men: they make broad their phylacteries and enlarge the borders of their garments.

6: And love the uppermost rooms at feasts, and the chief seats in the house.

7: And greetings in the markets, and to be called of men, Rabbi, Rabbi.

Now to the next verse of the parable.

Luke 16:20 And there was a certain beggar named Lazarus, which was laid at his gate, full of sores.

The beggar Lazarus being a Judaean who believed in the Messiah and his teachings.

Now to the next verse of the parable:

Luke 16:21 And desiring to be fed with the crumbs which fell from the rich man's table; moreover the dogs came and licked his sores.

The crumbs being the prophecies on the Messiah, whom the Pharisees rejected because they still went by the law of Moses. But the believing Israelite was willing to accept what was rejected by the other Jews and to be fed with these crumbs, for in them was eternal life.

Compare Luke 16:21 (above) with Matt. 15:26-27 (below), and notice that Lazarus the believing Jew was having his wounds licked by a dog.

The dog being the Gentiles, even though salvation was not to them yet. The dog was licking Lazarus's wounds because it wanted what he was getting, the crumbs. But as a believing Jew, Lazarus was treated like a dog, a Gentile, by the Jews who did not believe in the Messiah.

The following scriptures on the Canaanite woman who was a Gentile show better the meaning of the above scripture:

Matthew 15:23-28

23: But he answered her not a word. And his disciples came and besought him, saying, Send her away; for she crieth after us.

24: But he answered and said, I am not sent but unto the lost sheep of the house of Judaea.

25: Then came she and worshipped him, saying, Master, help me.

26: But he answered and said, It is not meet to take the children's bread, and to cast it to dogs.

27: And she said, Truth, Master: yet the dogs eat of the crumbs which fall from their masters' table.

28: Then Immanuel answered and said unto her, O woman, great is thy faith: be it unto thee even as thou wilt. And her daughter was made whole from that very hour.

This woman was willing to accept the crumbs. She also knew there was life in them.

Now to the next few verses of the parable.

Many teach that this is not a parable but that it actually happened. The ones that do, don't understand the resurrections or judgment and when the lake of fire actually takes place.

Luke 16:22-24

22: And it came to pass, that the beggar died, and was carried by the

Messengers into Abraham's bosom: the rich man also died and was buried;

23: And in the lake of fire he lift up his eyes, being in torments, and seeth Abraham afar off, and Lazarus in his bosom.

24: And he cried and said, Father Abraham, have mercy on me, and send Lazarus, that he may dip the tip of his finger in water, and cool my tongue; for I am tormented in this flame.

NOTE: If someone was in the Lake of Fire, they would need more than a tip of a finger for water, and no one would be holding a conversation if they were burning up.

These verses show the last state of these two. Lazarus went to Abraham's bosom. We'll show why it's called Abraham's bosom in the next verses.

Gal. 3:7, 28 & 29

7: Know ye therefore that they which are of faith, the same are the children of Abraham.

28: There is neither Jew nor Greek, there is neither bond nor free, there is neither male nor female: for ye are all one in the Messiah Yahweh.

29: And if ye be the Messiah's, then are ye Abraham's seed, and heirs according to the promise.

The rich man went to the lake of fire. Why?

Matt. 23:15-33

15: Woe unto you, scribes and Pharisees, hypocrites! for ye compass sea and land to make one proselyte, and when he is made, ye make him twofold more the child of the lake of fire than yourselves.

16: Woe unto you, ye blind guides, which say, Whosoever shall swear by the house it is nothing; but whosoever shall swear by the gold of the house, he is a debtor!

17: Ye fools and blind: for whether is greater, the gold, or the house that makes pure the gold?

18: And, Whosoever shall swear by the table, it is nothing: but whosoever sweareth by the gift that is upon it, he is guilty.

19: Ye fools and blind: for whether is greater, the gift, or the table that makes pure the gift?

20: Whoso therefore shall swear by the table, sweareth by it, and by all things thereon.

21: And whoso shall swear by the house, sweareth by it, and by him that dwelleth therein.

22: And he that shall swear by heaven, sweareth by the throne of Yahweh, and by Him that sitteth thereon.

23: Woe unto you, scribes and Pharisees, hypocrites! for ye pay tithe of mint and anise and cummin, and have omitted the weightier matters of the law, judgment, mercy, and a faith: these ought ye to have done, and not to leave the other undone.

24: Ye blind guides, which strain at a gnat, and swallow a camel.

25: Woe unto you, scribes and Pharisees, hypocrites! for ye make clean the outside of the cup and of the platter, but within they are full of extortion and excess.

26: Thou blind Pharisee, cleanse first that which is within the cup and platter, that the outside of them may be clean also.

27: Woe unto you, scribes and Pharisees, hypocrites! for ye are like unto whited sepulchres, which indeed appear beautiful outward, but are within full of dead men's bones, and of all uncleanness.

28: Even so ye also outwardly appear righteous unto men, but within ye are full of hypocrisy and iniquity.

29: Woe unto you, scribes and Pharisees, hypocrites! because ye build the tombs of the prophets, and garnish the sepulchres of the righteous.

30: And say, If we had been in the days of our fathers, we would not have been partakers with them in the blood of the prophets.

31: Wherefore ye be witnesses unto yourselves that ye are the children of them which killed the prophets.

32: Fill ye up then the measure of your fathers.

33: Ye serpents, ye generation of vipers, how can ye escape the damnation of the lake of fire.

Now, let's go to the next verse of the parable:

Luke 16:25 But Abraham said, Son, remember that thou in thy lifetime receivedst thy good things, and likewise Lazarus evil things: but now he is comforted, and thou art tormented.

We already know why the rich man received the good things from the first verse of this parable. Now, let us find out why Lazarus received evil things.

2 Timothy 3:12 Yea, and all that will live righteously in the Messiah Yahweh shall suffer persecution.

Acts 8:1-4

1: And Saul was consenting unto his death. And at that time there was a great persecution against the assembly which was at Zion; and they were all scattered abroad throughout the regions of Judaea and Samaria, except the apostles.

2: And devout men carried Stephen to his burial, and made great lamentation over him.

3: As for Saul, he made havoc of the called out ones, entering into every house, and hailing men and women committed them to prison.

4: Therefore, they that were scattered abroad went everywhere teaching the word.

Luke 16:26 And beside all this, between us and you there is a great gulf fixed: so that they which would pass from hence to you cannot; neither can they pass to us, that would come from thence.

The Great GULF, which either side, those burning in the Lake of Fire and those who are with Yahweh, cannot go to each other. Yahweh's people are going to be taken into spacecraft. They will be in heaven above earth praising Yahweh as the smoke of the Lake of Fire goes upward toward them.... So the GULF is the space between the spacecraft and the earth.

Now, let's go to the next few verses of the parable:

Luke 16:27-28

27: Then he said, I pray thee therefore; father, that thou wouldest <u>send him to my Father's House</u>:

(House of Yahweh):

28: For I have five brethren; that he may testify unto them, lest they also come into this place of torment.

Jeremiah 7:11 <u>Is this House, which is called by my name (YAHWEH)</u>, become a den of robbers in your eyes? Behold, even I have seen it, <u>saith Yahweh</u>.

Luke 16:29-30

29. **But Abraham replied "They have Moses and the prophets; let your brothers listen to them."**

30. **"No, father Abraham,' he said, 'but if someone is sent to them from the dead, they will repent."**

John 5:46-47

46. **If you had believed Moses, you would believe Me, because he wrote about Me.**

47. **But since you do not believe what he wrote, how will you believe what I say?"**

Who are these 5 brethren the rich man spoke of? We'll find out in the following scriptures.

Remember the one in the lake of fire was a Pharisee.

Pharisee being the one in the Lake of Fire.

- Scribes
- Sadducees
- Elders
- High Priests
- Chief Priest

Now, to prove that these were his brothers.

Matthew 16:21 From that time forth began Immanuel to show unto his disciples, <u>how that he must go unto Zion, and suffer many things of</u> the elders and chief priests and scribes, and be killed, and be <u>raised again the third day.</u>

Luke 24:18-20

[18] And the one of them, whose name was Cleopas, answering said unto him, Art thou only a stranger in Zion, and hast not known the things which are come to pass there in these days?

[19] And he said unto them, What things? And they said unto him, Concerning Immanuel of Nazareth, which was a prophet mighty in deed and word before Yahweh and all the people:

[20] And **<u>how the chief priests and our rulers delivered him to be condemned to death, and have killed him.</u>**

Matthew 16:12 Then understood they how that he bade them not beware of the leaven of bread, but of the doctrine of the Pharisees and of the Sadducees.

Luke 9:22 Saying, <u>The Son of man must suffer many things, and be rejected of</u> the elders and chief priests and scribes, <u>and be slain</u>, and be <u>raised the third day</u>.

Matthew 23:13 But woe unto you, scribes and Pharisees, hypocrites! for <u>ye shut up the kingdom of heaven against men: for ye neither go in yourselves, neither suffer ye them that are entering to go in.</u>

Mark 14:1 After two days was the feast of the passover, and of unleavened bread: and the chief priests and the scribes <u>sought how they might take him by craft, and put him to death.</u>

Matthew 26:2-4

2: Ye know that after two days is the feast of the passover, and the Son of man is betrayed to be killed.

3: <u>Then assembled together</u> the chief priests, and the scribes, and the elders of the people, unto the palace of the high priest, who was called Caiaphas,

4: <u>And consulted that they might take Immanuel by subtilty, and kill him.</u>

Matthew 26:57-67

57: And <u>they that had laid hold on Immanuel led him away</u>   to Caiaphas the high priest where the scribes and the elders were assembled.

58: But Peter followed him afar off unto the high priest's palace, and went in, and sat with the servants, to see the end.

59: Now the chief priests, and elders, and <u>all the council, sought false witness against Immanuel, to put him to death;</u>

60: But found none: yea, though many false witnesses came, yet found they none. At the last came two false witnesses.

61: And said, This fellow said, I am able to destroy the House of Yahweh, and to build it in three days.

63: But Immanuel held his peace. And the high priest answered and said unto him, I adjure thee by the living Yahweh, that thou tell us whether thou be the Messiah, the Son of Yahweh.

64: Immanuel saith unto him, Thou hast said: nevertheless I say unto you, Hereafter shall ye see the Son of man sitting on the right hand of power, and coming in the clouds of heaven.

65: Then the high priest rent his clothes, saying, He hath spoken blasphemy; what further need have we of witnesses? behold, now ye have heard his blasphemy.

66: What think ye? They answered and said, He is guilty of death.

67: Then did THEY spit in his face, and buffeted him; and other smote him with the palms of their hands,

Note: Not the Romans or soldiers, but the hierarchy of the House of Yahweh.

Matthew 27:1-2

1: When the morning was come, all the chief priests and elders of the people took counsel against Immanuel to put him to death:

2: And when they had bound him, they led him away, and delivered him to Pontius Pilate the governor.

Luke 24:20 And how the chief priests and our rulers <u>delivered him to be condemned to death and have crucified / KILLED him.</u>

John 18: 33-40

33. **Then Pilate entered into the judgment hall again, and called** Immanuel, **and said unto him, Art thou the King** of the Jews?

34. **Immanuel answered him, Sayest thou this thing of thyself, or did others tell it thee of me? 35. Pilate answered, Am I a Jew? <u>Thine own nation and the chief priests have delivered thee unto me</u>: what hast thou done?**

36. **Immanuel answered, My kingdom is not of this world: <u>if my kingdom were of this world, then would my servants fight, that I should not be delivered to the Jews:</u> but now is my kingdom not from hence.**

37. **Pilate therefore said unto him, Art thou a king then? Immanuel answered, Thou sayest that I am a king.**

To this end was I born, and for this cause came I into the world, that I should bear witness unto the truth.

Every one that is of the truth heareth my voice.

38. **Pilate saith unto him, What is truth? And when he had said this, he went out again unto the Jews, and saith unto them, I find in him no fault at all.**

39. **But ye have a custom, that I should release unto you one at the Passover: will ye therefore that I release unto you the King of the Jews?**

40. **Then cried they all again, saying, not this man, but Barabbas. Now Barabbas was a robber.**

John 19:6-8

6. **As soon as the chief priests and officers saw Him, they shouted, "Kill Him! Kill Him!" "Take Him and impale / KILL Him yourselves," Pilate replied, "For I find no basis for a charge against Him."**

7. **The Jews answered him, <u>We have a law, and by our law he ought to die</u>, because he made himself the Son of Yahweh.**

8. **When Pilate therefore heard that saying, he was the more afraid;**

John 19:10

10. **Then saith Pilate unto him, Speakest thou not unto me? knowest thou not that I have power to impale / KILL thee, and have power to release thee?**

11. **Immanuel answered, Thou couldest have no power at all against me, except it were given thee from above: therefore <u>he that delivered me unto thee hath the greater transgression</u>**

12. **And from thenceforth Pilate sought to release him: but the Jews cried out, saying, If thou <u>let</u> this man go, thou art not Caesar's friend: <u>whosoever maketh himself a king speaketh against Caesar.</u>**

13. **When Pilate therefore heard that saying, he brought Immanuel forth, and sat down in the judgment seat in a place that is called the Pavement, but in the Hebrew, Gabbatha.**

14. **And it was the preparation of the passover, and about the sixth hour: and he saith unto the Jews, Behold your King!**

15. **But they cried out, Away with him, away with him, kill him. Pilate saith unto them, "<u>Shall I impale / KILL your King?</u>" The chief priests answered, "We have no king but Caesar."**

16. **Then delivered he him therefore unto them to be KILLED.**

And they took Immanuel and led him away.

And he bearing his yoke went forth into a place called the place of a skull, which is called in the Hebrew: Golgotha.

17. **Where they killed him, and two other with him,** on either side one, and Immanuel in the midst.

Mark 8:31

And he began to teach them, <u>that the Son of man must suffer many things</u>, and <u>be rejected of </u>the elders, and of the chief priests, and scribes, <u>and be killed, and after three days rise again.</u>

John 18:31

31 Then said Pilate unto them, Take ye him, and judge him according to your law. The Jews therefore said unto him, It is not lawful for us to put any man to death:

Why was this? Because they were under Roman Authority and Law, they could not put someone to death; only Rome could put someone to death. But Pilate gave Immanuel over to the Jews and told them to kill him. So, by Jewish Law, they did just that.

John 19:19-22 "And Pilate wrote a title and put it on the TREE. <u>And the writing was, IMMANUEL OF NAZARETH, THE KING OF THE JEWS. Then many of the Jews read this title, for the place where Immanuel was killed was near the city, and it was written in Hebrew. (THIS PART WAS ADDED: "and Greek, and Latin.) Then the chief priests of the Jews said to Pilate, Do not write, the king of the Jews, but that he said, I am king of the Jews. Pilate answered, What I have written I have written."</u>

Pilate wrote a title and put it on the TREE. And the writing was IMMANUEL OF NAZARETH, THE KING OF THE JEWS. So, Pilate actually knew Hebrew to write that, and the Jews read it in their language. Then, many of the Jews read this title, for the place where Immanuel was killed was near the city, and it was written in Hebrew. Pilate answered, What I have written, I have written." So he personally wrote it himself.

<u>Latin was the original language of the Romans and remained the language of imperial administration, legislation, and the military throughout the classical period, and *the common person did not know Latin.*</u>

Acts 5:17-18

17: Then the high priest rose up, and all they that were with him, (which is the sect of the Sadducees,) and were filled with indignation,

18: And <u>laid their hands on the apostles, and put them in the common prison.</u>

Acts 5:27-28

27: And <u>when they had brought them, they set them before the council:</u> and the high priest asked them,

28: Saying, <u>Did not we straitly command you that ye should not teach in this name?</u> and, behold, <u>ye have filled Zion with your doctrine, and intend to bring this man's blood upon us.</u>

Why was this? Because they were under Roman Authority and Law, so they could not put someone to death; only Rome could put someone to death. But Pilate gave Immanuel over to the Jews and told them to kill him. So, by Jewish Law, they did just that.

NOTE: After reading all these, you're wondering how these are his brethren? There are four reasons why and they are:

1: They did not accept the prophecies of the coming Messiah.

2: They were all responsible for the death of the Messiah.

3: They persecuted the Judaeans that believed in the Messiah.

4: They all tried to stop the spread of the truth of the Messiah.

CHAPTER 25

DEATH:

You must understand death before you can understand the Resurrections.

What happens when you die? Do you go to heaven or the Christian Hell? Let's find out.

Ecclesiastes 3:21 Who knoweth the spirit of man that goeth upward, and the spirit of the beast that goeth downward to the earth?

Ecclesiastes 9:5-6,10

5 For the living know that they shall die but the dead know not anything, neither have they any more a reward; for the memory of them is forgotten.

6 Also their love, and their hatred, and their envy, is now perished; neither have they any more a portion for ever in any thing that is done under the sun.

10 **Whatsoever thy hand findeth to do, do it with thy might**; for there is no work, nor device, nor knowledge, nor wisdom, in the grave, whither thou goest.

Ecclesiastes 12: 7 **Then shall the dust return to the earth as it was**: and **the spirit shall return unto Yahweh who gave it.**

Job 3:11-19

11 "Why did I not perish at birth, and die as I came from the womb?

12 Why were there knees to receive me and breasts that I might be nursed?

13 **For now I would be lying down in peace; I would be asleep and at rest**

14 with kings and rulers of the earth, who built for themselves places now lying in ruins,

15 with princes who had gold, who filled their houses with silver.

16 **Or why was I not hidden away in the ground like a stillborn child, like an infant who never saw the light of day?**

17 **There the wicked cease from turmoil, and there the weary are at rest.**

18 Captives also enjoy their ease; they no longer hear the slave driver's shout.

19 **The small and the great are there, and the slaves are freed from their owners.**

Job 7:21

Why do you not pardon my offenses and forgive my transgressions? For I will soon lie down in the dust; you will search for me, but I will be no more."

Job 14:12 **So man lieth down, and riseth not: till the heavens be no more, they shall not awake, nor be raised out of their sleep.**

Job 21:23-33

23   **One dieth in his full strength, being wholly at ease and quiet.**

24   **His breasts are full of milk, and his bones are moistened with marrow. 25 And another dieth in the bitterness of his soul, and never eateth with pleasure.**

26 **They shall lie down alike in the dust, and the worms shall cover them.**

27 Behold, I know your thoughts, and the devices *which* ye wrongfully imagine against me.

28 For ye say, Where *is* the house of the prince? and where *are* the dwelling places of the wicked?

29 Have ye not asked them that go by the way? and do ye not know their tokens,

30 That the wicked is reserved to the day of destruction? they shall be brought forth to the day of wrath.

Psalms 13:3 "Consider and hear me, O Yahweh: lighten mine eyes, <u>lest I sleep the sleep of death;</u>"

Psalms 30:9. <u>"What profit is there in my blood, when I go down to the pit? Shall the dust praise thee? shall it declare thy truth?</u>"

<u>Psalms 49:14 "Like sheep they are laid in the grave; death shall feed on them; and the upright shall have dominion over them in the morning; and their beauty shall consume in the grave from their dwelling.</u>" Psalms 88:1-12

1 For my soul is full of troubles, And my life draws near to the grave.

4 I am counted with those who go down to the pit;

I am like a man *who has* no strength,

5 Adrift among the dead,

Like the slain who lie in the grave,

Whom You remember no more,

And who are cut off from Your hand. 6 You have laid me in the lowest pit, In darkness, in the depths.

7 Your wrath lies heavy upon me,

And You have afflicted *me* **with all Your waves.** *Selah*

8 **You have** [e]**put away my acquaintances far from me;**

You have made me an abomination to them;

I am **shut up, and I cannot get out;**

9 **My eye wastes away because of affliction. LORD, I have called daily upon You;**

I have stretched out my hands to You.

10 **Will You work wonders for the dead?**

Shall [f]**the dead arise** *and* **praise You?** *Selah*

11 **Shall Your lovingkindness be declared in the grave?**

Or **Your faithfulness in the place of destruction?**

12 **Shall Your wonders be known in the dark?**

And Your righteousness in the land of forgetfulness?

Psalms 89:48 <u>What man is he that liveth, and shall not see death? shall he deliver his soul from the hand of the grave?</u>

Psalms 104:29 Thou hidest thy face, they are troubled: thou takest away their breath, they die, and return to their dust.

Psalms 115:17 The dead praise not Yahweh, <u>neither any that go down into silence.</u>

<u>Psalms 143:3</u> For the enemy hath persecuted my soul; **he hath smitten my life down to the ground; he hath made me to dwell in darkness, as those that have been long dead.**

Psalms143:7 Hear me speedily, O Yahweh: my spirit faileth: **hide not thy face from me, lest I be like unto them that go down <u>into the pit</u>.**

Psalms 146:4 His breath goeth forth, he returneth to his earth; **in that very day his thoughts perish.**

Daniel 12:2 And many of them that sleep in the dust of the earth <u>shall awake, some to everlasting life, and some to shame and everlasting contempt.</u>

<u>Only Yahweh can kill the body and soul</u>. **That is why human death is called sleep. The true meaning of death is when Yahweh kills the body and soul, the breath of life, and the body makes a living soul. Yahweh will kill the body and soul of the wicked with the Lake of Fire, and they will never exist again!**

John 11:11 These things said he: and after that he saith unto them. Our friend Lazarus sleepeth; **but I go, that I may awake him out of sleep.**
4.

13   **Howbeit Immanuel spake of his death**: but they <u>thought that he had spoken of taking of rest in sleep.</u>

14   Then said Jesus unto them plainly, **<u>Lazarus is dead</u>**.

Acts 7:59-60 59 <u>And they stoned Stephen</u>, calling upon Yahweh, and saying, Yahweh, receive my spirit.

60 And he kneeled down, and cried with a loud voice, Yahweh, lay not this transgression to their charge. And when he had said this, <u>he fell asleep</u>.

Revelation 14:13 "And I heard a voice from heaven saying unto me, Write, Blessed are the dead which die in Yahweh from henceforth: Yea, saith the Spirit, that they may rest from their labors; and their works do follow them."

A DORMANT MIND IS DEATH TO KNOWLEDGE

"When you are uneducated about a subject, it is best to keep your mouth shut and open your mind. When you are educated on a subject, that is the time to open your mouth using your mind." by Gary Wendell Stanfield

CHAPTER 26

THE TWO THIEVES:

A. THIEF ON THE TREE - PART ONE:

Where did the thief go to?

Luke 23:32-43 - GIVES THE STORY

³² And there were also two other, malefactors, led with him to be put to death.

³³ And when they were come to the place, which is called Golgotha, there they impaled him, and the malefactors, one on the right hand, and the other on the left.

³⁴ Then said Immanuel, Father, forgive them; for they know not what they do. And they parted his raiment, and cast lots.

³⁵ And the people stood beholding. And the rulers also with them derided him, saying, He saved others; let him save himself, if he be king, the chosen of Yahweh.

³⁶ And the soldiers also mocked him, coming to him, and offering him vinegar,

³⁷ And saying, If thou be the king of the Jews, save thyself.

³⁸ And a superscription also was written over him in Hebrew, This Is The King Of The Jews.

GREEK AND LATIN WERE ADDED IN THIS VERSE. IT SHOULD ONLY BE WRITTEN IN HEBREW. GREEK WAS USED TO COVER UP THAT THE ORIGINAL "WORD OF YAHWEH" WAS DONE IN GREEK WHEN IT WAS

ORIGINALLY WRITTEN IN HEBREW. THE REASON FOR THE LATIN WORD IS THAT LATIN WAS THE LANGUAGE OF ROME, BUT THIS WAS ALL THE DOINGS OF THE HEBREW PEOPLE, AND THE ROMAN SOLDIERS JUST CARRIED OUT THE SENTENCE, SO THERE WAS NO NEED TO PUT IT IN LATIN. THE GREEKS AND ROMANS COULD HAVE CARED LESS ABOUT IMMANUEL'S DEATH; AFTER ALL, THEY WERE STILL PAGANS WITHOUT SALVATION AT THAT TIME.

³⁹ And one of the malefactors which were hanged railed on him, saying, If thou be king, save thyself and us.

⁴⁰ But the other answering rebuked him, saying, Dost not thou fear Yahweh, seeing thou art in the same condemnation?

⁴¹ And we indeed justly; for we receive the due reward of our deeds: but this man hath done nothing amiss.

⁴² And he said unto Immanuel, Master, remember me when thou comest into thy kingdom.

⁴³ And Immanuel said unto him, Verily I say unto thee **Today,** shalt thou be with me in paradise.

If we look at the above verse 43, it should read like this:

Same verse with comma put in the right place: And Immanuel said unto him, Verily I say unto **THEE,** today shalt thou be with me in paradise.

Matthew 12:40 For as Jonas was three days and three nights in the belly of the fish; so shall the Son of man be three days and three nights in the heart of the earth.

So, by this, the grave must be paradise. Not so. Paradise is the New Earth where there is no more death, no more tears, fears, and everlasting life living with Yahweh; that is paradise.

John 20:17 Immanuel saith unto her, Touch me not; for I am not yet ascended to my Father: but go to my brethren, and say unto them, I ascend unto my Father, and your Father;

By the above verse the Messiah said he had not ascended up to heaven yet.

John 3:13 And no man hath ascended up to heaven, but he that came down from heaven, *even* the Son of man which is in heaven.

By the above verse, we know no one had ascended to heaven only the son of man.

The scriptures did not have punctuations, chapters, or verses until the Middle Ages. Robert Estienne, a French printer, is given credit for verse divisions in his Greek Testament in 1551. Stephen Langston put chapters in the Latin Vulgate in 1228. A Dominican Monk, Paginus of Lucca, is credited with our present verse divisions of the Old Covenant. He used this verse system in his translation, which was printed in Latin in 1527.

To make verse 43 in Luke chapter 23 line up with scriptures you must move the comma as shown below in this verse.

43. And Immanuel said unto him, Verily I say unto thee **TODAY,** shalt thou be with me in paradise.

Notice the comma was moved from after THEE to after TODAY. The Messiah was telling him that he would be with him in paradise, but not on that day.

Below are some more examples where there was no comma or the comma was put in the wrong place, changing the meaning of the verses.

1 Corinthians 15:23 But every man in his own order: Messiah the first fruits; afterward they that are Yahweh's at his coming.

Same verse with a comma added to make it true: But every man in his own order: **MESSIAH,** the first fruits; afterward they that are Yahweh's at his coming.

Since he was the only one and the first fruit of those who slept.

Acts 26:23 That the Messiah should suffer, **and that he should be the first that should rise from the dead**, and should show light unto the people, and to the Gentiles.

Acts 19:12 So that from his body were brought unto the sick handkerchiefs or **APRONS,** and the diseases departed from them, and the evil spirits went out of them.

In the above verse, have you ever seen a sick handkerchief? Definitely not, so to make that verse read right, you must move the comma.

The same verse with the comma moved: So that from his body were brought unto **the SICK, handkerchiefs** or aprons and the diseases departed from them, and the evil spirits went out of them.

Mark 16:9 Now when Immanuel was risen early the first day of the **WEEK,** he appeared first to Mary Magdalene, out of whom he had cast seven devil.

Same verse with the comma moved: Now when Immanuel was **RISEN,** early the first day of the week, he appeared first to Mary Magdalene, out of whom he had cast seven Satan.

Immanuel was risen at the very end of the 7th Day Sabbath, not the first day of the week. So, to make this verse harmonize with the scriptures the comma must be moved once again.

Acts 3:26 Unto you first **YAHWEH,** having raised up his Son, sent him to bless you, in turning away every one of you from his iniquities.

Same verse with comma moved: Unto you **FIRST,** Yahweh having raised up his Son, sent him to bless you, in turning away every one of you from his iniquities.

1 Thessalonians 5:7 For they that **sleep sleep** in the night; and they that be drunken are drunken in the night.

Same verse with commas added: For they that **SLEEP,** sleep in the night; and they that be **DRUNKEN,** are drunken in the night.

JUST REMEMBER, MAN ADDED THE QUOTATION MARKS IN THE SCRIPTURES. THE THIEF WENT TO THE GRAVE AND NOWHERE ELSE AND IS STILL THERE TODAY.

B. THIEF ON THE TREE - PART TWO

Many will say about the thief on the tree that he was never baptized or filled with the Spirit with the evidence of speaking in tongues, so if he did not need it, why should we?

Let us go to the scriptures and find out why he did not need it:

Luke 23:32-43 - GIVES THE STORY

32   And there were also two other, malefactors, led with him to be put to death.

33   And when they were come to the place, which is called Golgotha, there they impaled him, and the malefactors, one on the right hand, and the other on the left.

34   Then said Immanuel, Father, forgive them; for they know not what they do. And they parted his raiment, and cast lots.

³⁵ And the people stood beholding. And the rulers also with them derided him, saying, He saved others; let him save himself, if he be king, the chosen of Yahweh.

³⁶ And the soldiers also mocked him, coming to him, and offering him vinegar,

³⁷ And saying, If thou be the king of the Jews, save thyself.

³⁹ And one of the malefactors which were hanged railed on him, saying, If thou be king, save thyself and us.

⁴⁰ But the other answering rebuked him, saying, Dost not thou fear Yahweh, seeing thou art in the same condemnation?

⁴¹ And we indeed justly; for we receive the due reward of our deeds: but this man hath done nothing amiss.

⁴² And he said unto Immanuel, Master, remember me when thou comest into thy kingdom.

⁴³ And Immanuel said unto him, Verily I say unto thee, today shalt thou be with me in paradise.

Now to show you why he did not need the infilling of Yahweh's Spirit. For the New Covenant to be established, the Messiah had to first be killed.

Luke 22:20 "This cup which is poured out for you is the NEW COVENANT in my blood."

Hebrews 9:26-28

²⁶ For then must he often have suffered since the foundation of the world: but now once in the end of the world hath he appeared to put away transgression by the offering of himself.

²⁷ And as it is appointed unto men once to die, but after this the judgment:

[28] So the Messiah was once offered to bear the transgressions of many; and unto them that look for him shall he appear the second time without transgression unto salvation.

The Spirit of Yahweh was not yet given, as you will see in the next scripture:

John 7:38-39

38.He that believeth on me, as the scripture hath said, out of his belly shall flow rivers of living water.

39.But this spake he of the Spirit, which they that believe on him should receive: for the Spirit was not yet given; because that Immanuel was not yet esteemed.

As you can see, the New Covenant was not yet established until the Messiah died and rose from the dead with the promise of the infilling of the Spirit of Yahweh., for those who would believe, which started on the day of Pentecost.

The thief was considered as still being under the Old Covenant and would not have had to have the Spirit infilling at that time.

CHAPTER 27

A. YAHWEH MESSIAH KILLED

1. THE LAST DAY MESSAGE THAT WILL TURN THE WORLD UPSIDE DOWN ONE LAST TIME.

John 1:1 IN THE BEGINNING WAS THE WORD, AND THE WORD WAS WITH YAHWEH, AND THE WORD WAS YAHWEH.

1 Timothy 3:16 And without controversy great is the mystery of righteousness: YAHWEH WAS MANIFEST IN THE FLESH, justified in the Spirit, seen of Messengers, taught unto the Gentiles, believed on in the world, received up into heaven.

Colossians 1:15-17,19

15. WHO IS THE IMAGE OF THE INVISIBLE YAHWEH, the first born of all creation;

16. FOR IN HIM WERE ALL THINGS CREATED, IN THE HEAVENS AND UPON THE EARTH, THINGS VISIBLE, INVISIBLE, WHITHER THRONES OR DOMINIONS OR PRINCIPALITIES OR POWERS; ALL THINGS HAVE BEEN CREATED THROUGH HIM, AND TO HIM.

17. AND HE IS BEFORE ALL THINGS, AND IN HIM ALL THINGS CONSIST.

19. FOR IT WAS THE GOOD PLEASURE OF THE FATHER THAT IN HIM SHOULD ALL THE FULNESS DWELL;

Colossians 2:9 FOR IN HIM DWELLETH ALL THE FULNESS OF YAHWEH BODILY.

2 John 1:7 For MANY DECEIVERS ARE ENTERED INTO THE WORLD, WHO CONFESS NOT THAT YAHWEH IS COME IN THE FLESH. THIS IS A DECEIVER AN ANTI-MESSIAH.

Acts 18:28 For he mightily convinced the Jews, and that publicly, SHOWING BY THE SCRIPTURES THAT YAWHEH WAS THE MESSIAH.

Luke 2:11 For unto you is born this day in the city of David a Savior, WHICH IS MESSIAH YAHWEH.

Matthew 16:20 Then he ordered his disciples not to tell anyone that he was the Messiah.

Acts 17:3 Opening and alleging that the Messiah must needs have suffered, and risen again from the dead; and THAT THIS IMMANUEL, WHOM I PREACH UNTO YOU, IS YAHWEH.

1 Corinthians 1:23 But WE PREACH YAHWEH KILLED, UNTO THE HEBREWS A STUMBLING BLOCK AND UNTO THE GENTILES FOOLISHNESS;

Isaiah 2:10-11

10.   Enter into the rock, and hide thee in the dust, for fear of Yahweh, and for the esteem of his majesty.

11.   The lofty looks of man shall be humbled, and the haughtiness of men shall be bowed down, and YAHWEH ALONE SHALL BE EXALTED IN THAT DAY.

Revelation 6:15-17

15.Then the kings of the earth, the princes, the generals, the rich, the mighty, and every slave and every free man hid in caves and among the rocks of the mountains. They called to the mountains and the rocks, "Fall on us and

16.And said to the mountains and rocks, Fall on us, and HIDE US FROM

THE FACE OF HIM WHO SITTETH ON THE THRONE AND FROM THE WRATH OF THE LAMB!

17.FOR THE GREAT DAY OF HIS WRATH HAS COME, AND WHO SHALL STAND?

John 3:36 He that believeth on the Son hath everlasting life: and he that believeth not the Son shall not see life; BUT THE WRATH OF YAHWEH ABIDETH ON HIM.

Revelation 1:8 I AM THE ALPHA AND THE OMEGA," SAYS THE SOVEREIGN YAHWEH, WHO IS AND WHO WAS AND WHO IS TO COME, YAHWEH.

Psalms 83:16-18

16. Fill their faces with shame; THAT THEY MAY SEEK THY NAME, O YAHWEH.

17.Let them be confounded and troubled forever; yea, let them be put to shame, and perish:

18.THAT MEN MAY KNOW THAT THOU, WHOSE NAME ALONE IS YAHWEH, ART THE MOST HIGH OVER ALL THE EARTH.

Malachi 2: 16 THEN THEY THAT FEARED YAHWEH SPOKE ONE WITH ANOTHER; AND YAHWEH LISTENED, AND HEARD, AND A BOOK OF REMEMBRANCE WAS WRITTEN BEFORE HIM, FOR THEM THAT FEARED YAHWEH, AND THAT THOUGHT UPON HIS NAME.

Isaiah 43:11 I, EVEN I, AM YAHWEH; AND BESIDE ME THERE IS NO SAVIOR.

Ezekiel 34:23 And I WILL SET UP ONE SHEPHERD OVER THEM, and HE SHALL FEED THEM, even my servant David; HE SHALL FEED THEM, and HE SHALL BE THEIR SHEPHERD.

John 10:3-5

3.To Him the porter openeth; and THE SHEEP HEAR HIS VOICE: and HE CALLETH HIS OWN SHEEP BY NAME, AND LEADETH THEM OUT.

4. And when HE PUTTETH FORTH HIS OWN SHEEP, HE GOETH BEFORE THEM, AND THE SHEEP FOLLOW HIM:

5. And a stranger will they not follow, but will flee from him: for they know not the voice of strangers.

Hebrews 4:12,13

12.For the word of Yahweh is quick, and powerful, and sharper than any two edged sword, piercing even to the dividing asunder of soul and spirit, and of the joints and marrow, and is a discerner of the thoughts and intents of the heart.

13.Neither is there any creature that is not manifest in his sight: but all things are naked and opened unto the eyes of him with whom we have to do.

YAHWEH MESSIAH

Immanuel was born through the flesh of man.

Born of a virgin through the Father's plan.

He died on an Olive tree as the offered Lamb.

We know now, He is the great "I Am." Who

had died for the transgressions of man.

Yahweh Messiah, scriptures prove it's He.

He says, there is no Savior, besides Me.

He's the flesh of the Father can't you see?

He is the only one, that can set you free.

If only you would believe, that He, is He.

By Gary Stanfield

John 8:24,28

24. I said therefore unto you, that ye shall die in your transgressions: for if ye believe not that I am He (YAHWEH), ye shall die in your transgressions.

28. Then said Immanuel unto them, When ye have lifted up the Son of man, then shall ye know that I am He (YAHWEH), and that I do nothing of myself; but as my Father hath taught me, I speak these things.

2 Thessalonians 2:13

But we are bound to give thanks always to Yahweh for you, brethren beloved of Yahweh, because Yahweh hath from the beginning chosen you to salvation through infilling of the Spirit and belief of the truth:

B. WHAT BELIEVING IN THE SON REALLY TRULY MEANS:

THE BEGINNING TO THE END. READ AND LEARN.

NOTE: Many people will use the following verse to try and show they are saved. But what does this verse really mean?

John 3:16 For Yahweh so loved the world, that he gave his only begotten Son, that whosoever believeth in him should not perish, but have everlasting life.

It is overwhelming at the ignorance that is in the world that people don't even know who the Messiah really is. These scriptures prove who he is and his true name. People need to start opening their minds to what the scriptures are really saying instead of what they have been indoctrinated to believe. Do not just read these, study them,

Listen to what they are telling you and receive it with an open mind for you THINK you have eternal life.

John 5:39 Search the scriptures; for in them ye think ye have eternal life: and they are they which testify of me.

Luke 24:44,45

44.And He said to them, these are my words which I spoke to you, while I was yet with you, that all things must be fulfilled, which are written in the law of Moses, and the prophets, and the psalms, concerning me.

45.Then he opened their mind, that they might understand the Scriptures.

John 1:1-2

1. **In the beginning was the Word, and the Word WAS WITH Yahweh, and the Word WAS Yahweh.**

2. **The same was in the beginning with Yahweh.**

3. **All things were made by him; and without him was not any thing made that was made.**

4. **In him was life; and the life was the light of men.**

5. **And the light shineth in darkness; and the darkness comprehended it not.**

Proverbs proves John

C. YAHWEH POSSESSED ME IN THE BEGINNING OF HIS WAY, BEFORE HIS WORKS OF OLD.

Proverbs 8:22-36

23.**I was set up from everlasting, from the beginning, or ever the earth was.**

24.**When there were no depths, I was brought forth ; when there were no fountains abounding with water.**

25.**Before the mountains were settled , before the hills was I brought forth**

26.**While as yet He had not made the earth, nor the fields, nor the highest part of the dust of the world.**

27.**When He prepared the heavens, I was there: when he set a compass upon the face of the depth:**

28. When He established the clouds above: when he strengthened the fountains of the deep:

29. When He gave to the sea his decree, that the waters should not pass his commandment: when He appointed the foundations of the earth:

30. Then I was by Him, as one brought up with Him: and I was daily His delight, rejoicing always before Him;

31. Rejoicing in the habitable part of His earth; and my delights were with the sons of men.

32. Now therefore hearken unto Me, O ye children: for blessed are they that keep My ways.

33. Hear instruction, and be wise , and refuse it not.

34. Blessed is the man that heareth Me, watching daily at my gates, waiting at the posts of my doors.

35. For whoso findeth Me findeth life, and shall obtain favor of Yahweh.

36. But He that transgresseth against me wrongeth his own soul: all they that hate Me love death.

COLLOSIANS 1:17.

AND HE IS BEFORE ALL THINGS, AND IN HIM ALL THINGS CONSIST.

THE FIRST THING YAHWEH DID IN CREATION WAS TO MAKE FLESH FOR HIMSELF.

John 14:6-29

6. Immanuel saith unto him, I am the way, the truth, and the life: no man cometh unto the Father, but by me.

7. If ye had known me, ye should have known my Father also: and from henceforth ye know Him, and have seen Him.

8. Philip told him, "Master, show us the Father, and that will satisfy us."

9. Immanuel saith unto him, Have I been so long time with you, and yet hast thou not known me, Philip? he that hath seen me hath seen the Father; and how sayest thou then, Shew us the Father?

10.Believest thou not that I am in the Father, and the Father in me(SELF SAME SPIRIT)? the words that I speak unto you I speak not of myself: but the Father that dwelleth in me(THE SPIRIT), He doeth the works.

11 Believe me that I am in the Father, and the Father in me: or else believe me for the very works' sake.

12 Verily, verily, I say unto you, He that believeth on me, the works that I do shall he do also; and greater works than these shall he do; because I go unto my Father.

13 And WHATSOEVER YE SHALL ASK IN MY NAME, THAT WILL I DO, that the Father may be esteemed in the Son.

14. IF YE SHALL ASK ANYTHING IN MY NAME, I WILL DO IT.

15 If ye love me, keep my commandments.

16 And I will pray the Father, and he shall give you another Comforter, that he may abide with you for ever;

17 Even the Spirit of truth; whom the world cannot receive, because it seeth him not, neither knoweth him: but ye know him; for he dwelleth with you, and shall be in you.

18 I will not leave you comfortless: I will come to you.

19 Yet a little while, and the world seeth me no more; but ye see me: because I live, ye shall live also.

20 At that day ye shall know that I am in my Father, and ye in me, and I in you.

21 He that hath my commandments, and keepeth them, he it is that loveth Me: and he that loveth Me shall be loved of my Father, and I will love him, and will manifest myself to him.

22 Judas saith unto him, not Iscariot, Master, how is it that thou wilt manifest thyself unto us, and not unto the world?

23 Immanuel answered and said unto him, If a man love me, he will keep my words: and my Father will love him, and we will come unto him, and make our abode with him.

24 He that loveth me not keepeth not my sayings: and the word which ye hear is not mine, but the Father's which sent me.

25 These things have I spoken unto you, being yet present with you.

26 But the Comforter, which is the Spirit, whom the Father will send in my name, he shall teach you all things, and bring all things to your remembrance, whatsoever I have said unto you.

27 Peace I leave with you, my peace I give unto you: not as the world giveth, give I unto you. Let not your heart be troubled, neither let it be afraid.

28 Ye have heard how I said unto you, I go away, and come again unto you. If ye loved me, ye would rejoice, because I said, I go unto the Father: for my Father is greater than I.

29 And now I have told you before it come to pass, that, when it is come to pass, ye might believe.

Philippians 2:6 Who, being in the form of Yahweh, thought it not robbery to be equal with Yahweh:

John 8:24,28

24. I said therefore unto you, that ye shall die in your transgressions: for if ye believe not that I am He (YAHWEH), ye shall die in your transgressions.

28. Then said Immanuel unto them, When ye have lifted up the Son of man, then shall ye know that I am He (YAHWEH), and that I do nothing of myself; but as my Father hath taught me, I speak these things.

D. WHY WAS THE MESSIAH KILLED?

John 11:46-48

46.But some of them went their ways to the Pharisees, and told them what things Immanuel had done.

47.Then gathered the chief priests and the Pharisees a council, and said, <u>What do we? for this man doeth many miracles.</u>

48.If we let him thus alone, <u>ALL MEN WILL BELIEVE IN HIM</u>: and the Romans shall come and <u>TAKE AWAY BOTH OUR PLACE AND NATION.</u>

Acts 4:26 THE <u>KINGS OF THE EARTH STOOD UP</u>, and <u>the rulers were gathered together against Yahweh, and against His Messiah.</u>

THIS HAPPENED ANYWAY TO THEM IN SPITE OF THEM KILLING THE MESSIAH. D. IMMANUEL DIED ON A REAL OLIVE TREE, NOT A CROSS:

Deuteronomy 21:23 <u>His body shall not remain all night upon the tree</u>, but thou shalt in any wise bury him that day; for he that is hanged is accursed of Yahweh; that thy land be not defiled, which Yahweh giveth thee for an inheritance.

Acts 5:30 Yahweh of our fathers raised up Immanuel, whom ye slew and <u>hanged on a tree.</u>

Acts 10:39 And we are witnesses of all things which he did both in the land of the Jews, and in Jerusalem; whom they slew and **hanged on a tree.**

Acts 13:30 And **when they had fulfilled all that was written of him**, **they took him down from the tree**, and laid him in a sepulcher.

1 Peter 2:24 <u>Who his own self bare our transgressions in his own body on the tree,</u> that we, being dead to transgressions, should live unto righteousness: by whose stripes ye were healed.

Galatians 3:13 Yahweh hath redeemed us from the curse of the law, being made a curse for us: for it is written, **Cursed is everyone that hangeth on a tree.**

John 19:31-33

31.Then the Jews, because it was the day of preparation, so **THAT THE BODIES WOULD NOT REMAIN ON THE TREE** on the Sabbath (for that Sabbath was a high [SPECIAL] day), asked Pilate that their legs might be broken, and that they might be taken away.

Notice the bodies, plural; would not remain on the tree, singular.

Now notice, it would be which way the soldiers went around the tree with who would have been next in line........to have the leg broken.

32.So the soldiers came, and broke the legs of the **first man and of the other who was impaled with him**;

33.but coming to Immanuel, when they saw that he was already dead, they did not break his legs....

John 19:18 Where **they killed him, and two others with him**, **one on either side, and Immanuel in the midst**.

Why didn't the soldiers go right down the line? If there were 3 different trees, or by Christian standards, Crosses. Because there was only one tree.

Mark 15: 27 And <u>**with him they impaled two thieves**</u>; the **one on his right hand, and the other on his left**.

Luke 23:29

29.For, behold, the days are coming, in the which they shall say, Blessed are the barren, and the wombs that never bare, and the paps which never gave suck.

[This is what's being said today.]

30.Then shall they begin to say to the mountains, Fall on us; and to the hills, Cover us.

[What people will say at Yahweh's return.]

31.<u>For if they do these things in a green tree</u>, what shall be done in the dry?

[Notice how he used a GREEN TREE when talking about the present back then and a dry when there would be no salvation. In other words he was saying if they are doing this with him there and the coming of salvation, what will people do when there is no salvation given. We are seeing what's happening in the world today without salvation, and it's only going to get worse.]

32.And there were also two other, malefactors, led with him to be put to death.

33.And when they were come to the place, which is called Golgotha there **<u>they impaled him, and the malefactors, one on the right hand, and the other on the left.</u>**

NOTE: All 3 were hung to the same tree. There were not 3 different ones, but the same tree. Otherwise the above scripture would have said, " **That the BODIES should not remain upon THE TREE.**" It would have been plural TREES if they all were hung on different trees, but they were all on the same tree.

In verse 32 of the above verses, it says the soldiers came and **broke the legs of the first and the other, which was IMPALED WITH HIM**.

Matthew 27:38 Then were the two thieves killed WITH HIM, one on the right hand, and another on the left.

NOTE: Nails in hands and feet are a lie. The only thing pierced was his side.

E. THIS HAPPENED ON A REAL TREE.

With the pagan word CROSS put into the scriptures, it makes it look like the scriptures teach that they all died on 3 different crosses, and the Messiah would have been on the middle one. Yet the centurion, instead of going down the line from left to right or right to left, breaking the legs, goes and breaks the legs of one of the thieves, then passes the middle cross that the Messiah was supposed to be on and breaks the legs of the second thief, then returns to the middle cross and the Messiah was already dead, and did not break his legs. When you put the true word TREE, then it makes sense how that it was just one tree and not 3 of them.

Note: The Messiah was killed on the Mount of Olives, so there must have been plenty of Olive trees for the Mount of Olives to be named that. Josephus relates that Titus cut down all the trees in the besiege of Jerusalem in 70 A.D.

They say that a Roman CROSS weighed 300 plus pounds. Which one person could never have been dragged through the streets of Jerusalem, as so many Christian pictures depict. Then others say it was the cross beam to the CROSS. Which is said to weigh 100 to 145 pounds. Only a physically fit person could carry that for any length of time. You must remember he was severely beaten, and other things were done to him that would make it physically impossible for him to carry a cross beam, even his physical stature. What was used, though, was some type of wood piece that might have been kind of heavy, and their arms were probably tied to it so a person could not escape by running off. It would wear a person out so that by the time they got to Golgotha they would be too worn out to even put up a fight. As scriptures show someone had to carry it for the Messiah because he was too weak and battered to even carry it very far.

Matthew 11:29 Take my **YOKE** upon you, and learn of me; for I am meek and lowly in heart: and ye shall find rest unto your souls.

Matthew 27: 31-32

31.And when they had mocked Him, they took the robe off Him, put His *own* clothes on Him, and led Him away to be killed.

32.Now as they came out, they found a man of Cyrene, Simon by name. Him they compelled to bear His cross / **YOKE**.

Galatians 5:1 Stand fast therefore in the liberty wherewith Yahweh hath made us free, and be not entangled again with the **YOKE** of bondage.

Jeremiah 27:2 Thus saith Yahweh to me; Make thee **BONDS and YOKES**, and put them upon thy neck,

Pilate told the Jews to kill him so his blood would be on their hands, which they did, and the Jews did not use a CROSS to execute but TREES. The Romans did not kill the Messiah. The Jews did. The Roman soldiers just made sure that the sentence was carried out. It was done under Jewish laws, not Roman law. The Lazarus and Rich Man parable proves that fact.

Matthew 27: 24-25

24.**When** Pilate saw that he was accomplishing nothing, but rather that a riot was starting, he took water and washed his hands in front of the crowd, saying, "I am innocent of this Man's blood; see to that yourselves."

25.And all the people said, "His blood shall be on us and on our children!"...

I have also been working on proving that where they put the word "CROSS," other words go there in their place. Here are some of the verses that are completed.

1 Corinthians 1:17-18

17.For Christ / **YAHWEH** sent me not to baptize, but to teach the gospel / **WORD**, not with wisdom of words, lest the cross of Christ **/ SPIRIT OF YAHWEH** should be made of non effect.

18.For the teaching of the cross **/ SPIRIT i**s to them that perish "foolishness", unto us which are saved it is the power of God / **YAHWEH**.

John 19:31 The Jews therefore, because it was the preparation, that the bodies should not remain upon the cross / **TREE** on the sabbath day, (for that sabbath day was an high day,) besought Pilate that their legs might be broken, and that they might be taken away.

Luke 9:23 And he said to them all, If any man will come after me, let him deny himself, and take up his cross / **YOKE** daily, and follow me.

Mark 10:21 Then Immanuel beholding him loved him, and said unto him, One thing thou lackest: go thy way, sell whatsoever thou hast, and give to the poor, and thou shalt have treasure in heaven: and come, take up the cross / **YOKE**, and follow me.

Matthew 10:38 And he that taketh not his cross / **YOKE**, and followeth after me, is not worthy of me.

Galatians 5: 11 And I, brethren, if I yet teach circumcision, why do I yet suffer persecution? then is the offence of the **cross/ Law ceased.**

Colossians 2:14 Blotting out the handwriting of ordinances that was against us, which was contrary to us, and took it out of the way, nailing it to his cross / **TREE**;

Colossians 1:20 And, having made peace through the blood of his cross / **FLESH**, by him to reconcile all things unto himself; by him, I say, whether they be things in earth, or things in heaven.

KILLED ON AN OLIVE TREE ON THE MOUNT OF OLIVES.

**PSALMS 52:8 But I am like a green olive tree in the 'House of YAHWEH':
I trust in the mercy and faithfulness of YAHWEH forever and ever.**

CHAPTER 28

DEATH AND RESURRECTION

- 3 DAYS AND 3 NIGHTS A FULL 72 HOUR PERIOD IN THE TOMB:

Starting off with what most of Christianity teaches the death and resurrection to be: They teach the last Supper as Holy Thursday, Holy has to do with the sun, then he was crucified on a cross (a sun symbol), the 6th day (Friday) "Good Friday." What is interesting about Christians calling that day "Good Friday," is if you look up Christ in paganism, it means "GOOD," which is a sun deity name. So, this is where they produced, calling it "Good" Friday. Then 36 hours (about 1 and a half days) later and not 72 hours (3 days), which makes up 3 full days, they say their Jesus (also a pagan sun deity name) was raised on the 1st day of the week (Sunday) the day the pagans worshiped the sun the Lord's Day, long before Christianity was started by Constantine who was a pagan sun worshiper, called Easter Sunday, the day before that is Holy Saturday, Yahweh's true Sabbath day. And named the day they are taught as the resurrection day "Easter," a pagan deity known for fertility, and thus the rabbit and chicken, which are also known for fertility. You can see by this paragraph just how much paganism is incorporated into the Christian belief system for what is called Holy Week.

Now for the truth to the Christian lies about the death and resurrection. Immanuel was hung by his wrists with rope on a real live Olive Tree according to Jewish Law and put in the tomb just before sundown of the same day (Wednesday Passover.) Back then the night part came first, then the day part as a day. Where this has been changed to the day starts at midnight and ends at midnight, 24 hours later.

The Hebrew day begins and ends at sunset, according to the scriptures and the practice of the Jews even today.

Gen 1:5 And Yahweh called the light Day and the darkness he called Night. And <u>the evening and the morning were the first day.</u>

Lev 23:32 ... <u>from even unto even</u>, shall ye celebrate your Sabbath.

Acts 12:4 And when he had apprehended him {Peter}, he put him in prison, and delivered him to four quaternions of soldiers to keep him; intending after <u>Easter</u> to bring him forth to the people.

King James replaced Passover with the word Easter. Constantine made sure that the Passover and Easter would never fall on the same day and that Easter would always be on a Sunday.

Immanuel would have been resurrected three days and nights later. His death and burial took place on the 4th day of the week (Wednesday). His burial took place at the end of the day, and he was raised at the end of the 7th day Sabbath (Saturday), not the 1st day of the week (Sunday), a full 72 hours later.

I'm only going to use the verses that bring out most of the truth or that add some more truth to what happened.

Matthew 12:40 For as Jonas was three days and three nights in the belly of the fish; so shall the Son of man be three days and three nights in the heart of the earth.

Jonah 1:17 Now Yahweh had prepared a great fish to swallow up Jonah. And Jonah was in the belly of the fish three days and three nights.

John 2:19 Immanuel answered and said unto them, Destroy this house, and in three days I will raise it up.

Matthew 20:19 And shall deliver him to the Gentiles to mock, and to scourge, and to kill him: and the third day he shall rise again.

The Romans nailed people to a cross and crucified them, but Pilot did not want Immanuel's blood on his hands, so he gave him over to the Jewish hierarchy to have them kill him. Thus, he was killed by the Jews and the Jewish Law, which was by being hung on a tree, and not by Roman Law, which would have been the cross. The Roman soldiers just made sure that the death sentence was carried out.

Matthew 16:21 From that time forth began Immanuel to shew unto his disciples, how that he must go unto Zion, and suffer many things of the elders and chief priests and scribes, and be killed, and be raised again the third day.

John 19:31 The Jews therefore, because it was the preparation, that the bodies should not remain upon the tree on the Sabbath day, (for that Sabbath day was a <u>HIGH DAY</u>, the first day of Unleavened Bread besought Pilate that their legs might be broken, and *that* they might be taken away. High Sabbath meant a Special Sabbath, that day (Wednesday) was a preparation day for the 1st day of Unleavened Bread, which would have been the very next day. (Thursday.

Leviticus 23:5-8

[5] In the <u>fourteenth day of the first month at even</u> <u>is Yahweh's Passover</u>.

⁶ And on <u>the fifteenth day of the same month is the feast of unleavened bread</u> unto Yahweh: seven days ye must eat unleavened bread.

⁷ In the first day ye shall have a <u>righteous convocation</u> {special Sabbath}: ye shall <u>do no servile work therein</u>.

⁸ But ye shall offer an offering made by fire unto Yahweh seven days: in <u>the seventh day is a righteous convocation</u> {special Sabbath}: <u>ye shall do no servile work therein</u>.

The Passover was preparation day for the Feast of Unleavened bread.

Exodus 12:18 In the first month, on the fourteenth day of the month at even, ye shall eat unleavened bread, until the one and twentieth day of the month at even.

Lev 23:5 In the fourteenth day of the first month at even is Yahweh's Passover.

John 19:14 And it was the preparation of the Passover, and about the sixth hour: and he saith unto the Jews, Behold your King!

John 19:19 And Pilate wrote a title, and put it on the tree. And the writing was Immanuel Of Nazareth The King Of The Jews.

Mark 15:22 And they bring him unto the place Golgotha, which is, being interpreted, The place of a skull.

Luke 23:38 And a superscription also was written over him in letters in Hebrew, This Is The King Of The Jews.

Greek and Latin were added to that verse and showed why in an earlier study in this book.

Mark 15:25 And it was the third hour, and they killed him.

Matthew 27:45 Now from the sixth hour there was darkness over all the land unto the ninth hour. Sixth Hour is 9 to 12 noon

Ninth Hour is 12 to 3 P.M.

Matthew 27: 50 Immanuel, when he had cried again with a loud voice, yielded up the Spirit.

John 19:38-40 - Twelfth Hour is 3 to 6 P.M.

38.And after this Joseph of Arimathaea, being a disciple of Immanuel, but secretly for fear of the Jews, besought Pilate that he might take away the body of Immanuel: and Pilate gave him leave. He came therefore, and took the body of Immanuel.

39.And there came also Nicodemus, which at the first came to Immanuel by night, and brought a mixture of myrrh and aloes, about an hundred pound weight.

40.Then took they the body of Immanuel, and wound it in linen clothes with the spices, as the manner of the Jews is to bury.

Notice that his body was wound in a linen cloth, not draped like the Shroud of Turin that shows the front and back, a fake on one cloth. The pagans called Sunday their day of worship for the sun, the Lord's Day, long before Christianity, was started by Constantine, who was a pagan sun worshiper.

Matthew 27:57-61

57.When the even was come, there came a rich man named Joseph, who also himself was Immanuel's disciple

58.He went to Pilate, and begged the body of Immanuel. Then Pilate commanded the body to be delivered

59.And when Joseph had taken the body, he wrapped it in a clean linen cloth,

60.And laid it in his own new tomb, which he had hewn out in the rock: and he rolled a great stone to the door of the sepulcher, and departed.

61.And there was Mary Magdalene, and the other Mary, sitting over against the sepulcher.

Luke 23:54-55

54.And that day was the preparation, and the Sabbath drew on.

55.And the women also, which came with him from Galilee, followed after, and beheld the sepulcher, and how his body was laid.

56.And they returned, and prepared spices and ointments; and rested the Sabbath day according to the commandment.

Matthew 27:63-64

63.Saying, Sir, we remember that that deceiver said, while he was yet alive, After three days I will rise again.

64.Command therefore that the sepulcher be made sure until the third day, lest his disciples come by night, and steal him away, and say unto the people, He is risen from the dead: so the last error shall be worse than the first.

65.Pilate said unto them, YE HAVE A WATCH: GO YOUR WAY, MAKE IT AS SURE AS YOU CAN.

66.So they went, and made the sepulcher sure, sealing the stone, and SETTING A WATCH AT THE END OF THE SABBATH.

The end of a Sabbath WATCH would be from 3 to 6 P.M., at the night time ending hours of the Sabbath Day.

A WATCH is at night. An HOUR is during the day.

12 mid - Roman start of day | Jewish 6th hour night

3:00am - Roman 3rd hour | Jewish 9th hour of night

6:00am - Roman 6th hour | Jewish start of day (sunrise)

9:00am - Roman 9th hour | Jewish 3rd hour day

12 noon - Roman 12th hour | Jewish 6th hour day

3:00pm - Roman 3rd hour | Jewish 9th hour day

6:00pm - Roman 6th hour | Jewish 12th hour (sunset)

9:00pm - Roman 9th hour | Jewish 3rd hour of night

1st WATCH Third Hour is 6 to 9 A.M - 3-hour intervals

2nd WATCH Sixth Hour is 9 to 12 noon 3rd

WATCH Ninth Hour is 12 to 3 P.M.

4th WATCH Twelfth Hour is 3 to 6 P.M.

Mark 16:1-2

1. And **WHEN THE SABBATH WAS PAST**, Mary Magdalene, and Mary the mother of James, and Salome, had bought sweet spices, that they might come and anoint him.

2. **And very early in the morning on the first day of the week, they came unto the sepulcher at the rising of the sun.**

Mark 16:9 Now when Immanuel was **RISEN**, early the first day of the week, he appeared first to Mary Magdalene, out of whom he had cast seven devils.

In above verse 9, a point must be made here. Punctuations were put into the scriptures by man. They should have put a COMMA after RISEN, too.

So that verse should read: Now when Immanuel was RISEN,< early the first day of the week, he appeared....... That way, the verse will line up with the rest of the scriptures in this study.

Luke 24:1-10,12

1. Now, upon the first day of the week, very early in the morning, they came unto the sepulcher, bringing the spices which they had prepared, and certain others with them.

² **And they found the stone rolled away from the sepulcher.**

³ **And they entered in and found not the body of the Master Yahweh.**

⁴ **And it came to pass, as they were much perplexed thereabout, behold, two men stood by them in shining garments:**

⁵ **And as they were afraid, and bowed down their faces to the earth, they said unto them, Why seek ye the living among the dead?**

⁶ **He is not here, but is risen: remember how he spoke unto you when he was yet in Galilee,**

⁹ **And returned from the sepulcher, and told all these things unto the eleven, and to all the rest.**

[10] It was Mary Magdalene and Joanna, and Mary the mother of James, and other women that were with them, which told these things unto the apostles.

[12] Then arose Peter, and ran unto the sepulcher; and stooping down, he beheld the linen clothes laid by themselves, and departed, wondering in himself at that which was come to pass.

CHAPTER 29

PAUL NOT A FALSE APOSTLE:

LATELY, I HAVE BEEN SEEING A LOT OF PEOPLE TEACHING THAT PAUL IS A FALSE APOSTLE, SO I AM ADDING MY STUDY ON PAUL TO PROVE THAT HE WAS NOT A FALSE APOSTLE. The Torah believers must realize that Yahweh did away with the letter of the Law and gave a better way that the Law could not do, and this was done by the infilling of the Spirit, which gave salvation without animal offerings to cover transgressions.

THE FOLLOWING COMMENT CAME FROM ANOTHER SITE, BUT THE PERSON HIT THE TRUTH RIGHT ON THE HEAD IT IS AS FOLLOWS: "Many have been deceived by men of scholar. As believers, we tend to look at a man's scholastic credentials or how many books they may have written to determine whether they are teaching truth."

There are so many things that Paul wrote about that I'm going to just bring out the things to prove that Paul was a true Apostle and not what a lot of these Torah people teach that Paul was not an Apostle but a False Apostle.

Matthew 10:2-5

2 Now the names of the twelve apostles are these; The first, Simon, who is called Peter, and Andrew his brother; James the son of Zebedee, and John his brother;

3 Philip, and Bartholomew; Thomas, and Matthew the publican; James the son of Alphaeus, and Lebbaeus, whose surname was Thaddaeus;

4 Simon the Canaanite, and Judas Iscariot, who also betrayed him.

Acts 1:26

26 And they gave forth their lots; and the lot fell upon Matthias; and he was numbered with the eleven apostles.

Immanuel picked the original 12. Then Judas did what he did, which left 11, so the disciples replaced Judas by picking straws or stones with Mathias.

Acts 1:21-23

21 Wherefore of these men which have companied with us all the time that Master Immanuel went in and out among us,

22 Beginning from the baptism of John, unto that same day that he was taken up from us, must one be ordained to be a witness with us of his resurrection.

23 And they appointed two, Joseph called Barsabas, who was surnamed Justus, and Matthias.

To be an Apostle one had to be with Him from His baptism unto His resurrection!

If there were 12, then Judas was no longer one, and they picked just 1 from the 2 to make 12 again.

Does Paul fit the requirements for being an Apostle? If he was not with the 12 from his baptism nor anytime during His ministry, nor witness his resurrection, how could he qualify?

Matthew 10:5 These twelve Immanuel sent forth, and commanded them, saying, Go NOT into the way of the Gentiles They were to go only to the lost tribes of Judaea.

Paul did not have to meet the requirements; the first 12 did.

HOW DID PAUL BECOME EXEMPT?

Paul was sent to the Gentiles and at first went to the lost House of Judaea, but his past persecutions of them made it impossible at the time, and why he went. He was sent to the Gentiles, and some 15 years later, he started teaching the Jews and Gentiles alike.

There are some who believe Peter was sent to the Gentiles. This happened just one time and for a reason. Being that Peter was one of the original 12 and sent to the Jews only, and Cornelius was the first Gentile and his family to receive salvation......This happened also to set Paul's Apostleship up.

Acts 15:6-8

6 And the apostles and elders came together for to consider of this matter.

7 And when there had been much disputing, Peter rose up, and said unto them, Men and brethren, ye know how that a good while ago Yahweh made choice among us, that the Gentiles by my mouth should hear the Word of Yahweh, and believe.

8 And Yahweh, which knoweth the hearts, bare them witness, giving them the Spirit, even as he did unto us;

This was done so Peter would go and tell the other disciples that the Gentiles were also given salvation. Here is Peter in the following verses commending Paul and his letters.

217

2A. PETER PRAISES PAUL:

2 Peter 3:13-17

13 Nevertheless we, according to His promise, look for new heavens and a new earth, wherein dwelleth righteousness.

14 Wherefore, beloved, seeing that ye look for such things, be diligent that ye may be found of him in peace, without spot, and blameless.

15 And account that the longsuffering of our Lord is salvation; even as our beloved brother Paul also according to the wisdom given unto him hath written unto you;

16 As also in all his letters, speaking in them of these things; in which are some things hard to be understood, which they that are unlearned and unstable wrest, as they do also the other scriptures, unto their own destruction.

17 Ye therefore, beloved, seeing ye know these things before, beware lest ye also, being led away with the error of the wicked, fall from your own steadfastness.

Matthew 24:24 For there will appear false Messiahs and false prophets performing great miracles — amazing things! — so as to fool even the chosen, if possible.

Galatians 1:1 "Paul, an apostle, (not of men, neither by man, BUT BY YAHWEH MESSIAH, AND YAHWEH THE FATHER, who raised him from the dead;)"

Romans 1:1,4

1. Paul, a servant of Yahweh Messiah, called [to be] an apostle, separated unto the Word of Yahweh,

5. By whom we have received favor and apostleship, for obedience to the faith among all nations, for his name:

16. For I am not ashamed of the Word of Yahweh: for it is the power of Yahweh unto salvation to every one that believeth; TO THE JEW FIRST, and ALSO TO THE GENTILE.

1 Corinthians 15:5-10

5. **And that he was seen of Cephas, then of the twelve:**

6. **After that, he was seen of above five hundred brethren at once; of whom the greater part remain unto this present, but some are fallen asleep.**

7. **After that, he was seen of James; then of all the apostles.**

8. **And LAST OF ALL HE WAS SEEN OF ME also, as of one born out of due time.**

9. **For I AM THE LEAST OF THE APOSTLES, that am not meet to be called an apostle, BECAUSE I PERSECUTED THE ASSEMBLY OF YAHWEH.**

10.**But by the favor of Yahweh I am what I am: and HIS SPIRIT WHICH WAS BESTOWED UPON ME WAS NOT IN VAIN; but I LABORED MORE ABUNDANTLY THAN THEY ALL: yet NOT I, BUT THE SPIRITI OF YAHWEH WHICH WAS WITH ME.**

3A. PAUL TRIBE OF BENJAMIN:

Romans 11:1 I say then, has Yahweh cast away His people? Certainly not! For I also am a Judaean, of the seed of Abraham, of the tribe of Benjamin.

4A. PAUL A PHARISEE:

Acts 23:6 Then Paul, knowing that some of them were Sadducees and others Pharisees, called out in the Sanhedrin, "Brothers, I am a Pharisee, the son of a Pharisee. It is because of my hope in the resurrection of the dead" that I am on trial.

5A. PAUL THE PERSECUTOR:

Acts 9:1-31

1 And Saul, yet breathing out threatenings and slaughter against the disciples of Yahweh, went unto the high priest,

2 And desired of him letters to Damascus to the assemblies, that if he found any of this way, whether they were men or women, he might bring them bound unto Zion.

6A. PAUL GIVEN SALVATION:

Spacecraft appears above Paul:

3. And as he journeyed, he came near Damascus: and suddenly there shined round about him a light from heaven:

4 And he fell to the earth, and heard a voice saying unto him, Saul, Saul, why persecutest thou me? 5 And he said, Who art thou, Master? And Yahweh said, I am Yahweh whom thou persecutest: it is hard for thee to kick against the pricks.

6 And he trembling and astonished said, Master, what wilt thou have me to do? And Yahweh said unto him, Arise, and go into the city, and it shall be told thee what thou must do.

7. And the men which journeyed with him stood speechless, hearing a voice, but seeing no man. 8 And Saul arose from the earth; and when his eyes were opened, he saw no man: but they led him by the hand, and brought him into Damascus.

9 And he was three days without sight, and neither did eat nor drink.

10 And there was a certain disciple at Damascus, named Ananias; and to him said Yahweh in a vision, Ananias. And he said, Behold, I am here, Master.

11 And Yahweh said unto him, Arise, and go into the street which is called Straight, and enquire in the house of Judas for one called Saul, of Tarsus: for, behold, he prayeth,

12 And hath seen in a vision a man named Ananias coming in, and putting his hand on him, that he might receive his sight.

13 Then Ananias answered, Master, I have heard by many of this man, how much evil he hath done to thy elect at Zion:

14 And here he hath authority from the chief priests to bind all that call on thy name.

15 But Yahweh said unto him, Go thy way: for HE IS A CHOSEN VESSEL UNTO ME, TO BEAR MY NAME BEFORE THE GENTILES, and kings, AND THE CHILDREN OF JUDAEA:

16 For I will shew him how great things he must suffer for my name's sake.

17 And Ananias went his way, and entered into the house; and putting his hands on him said, Brother Saul, Yahweh, that appeared unto thee in the way as thou camest, hath sent me, that thou mightest receive thy sight, and be filled with the Spirit.

18 And immediately there fell from his eyes as it had been scales: and he received sight forthwith, and arose, and was baptized.

19 And when he had received meat, he was strengthened. Then was Saul certain days with the disciples which were at Damascus.

20 And straightway <u>he taught Yahweh in the assemblies, that he is the Son of Yahweh.</u>

21 But all that heard him were amazed, and said; <u>Is not this he that destroyed them which called on this name in Zion,</u> and came hither for that intent, that he might bring them bound unto the chief priests?

Paul was taken from the House of Yahweh and was going to be killed by the Jews because of his teachings. He was taken out of the House, and the doors shut behind him.

Acts 21:28-39

28 Crying out, Men of Judaea, help: This is the man, **that teacheth all *men* <u>every where against the people, and the law, and this place:</u>** and further brought Greeks also into the **House**, and hath polluted this righteous place.

29 (For they had seen before with him in the city Trophimus an Ephesian, whom they supposed that Paul had brought into the House.)

30 And all the city was moved, and **<u>the people ran together: and they took Paul, and drew him out of the House: and forthwith the doors were shut.</u>**

31 And **<u>as they went about to kill him, tidings came unto the chief captain of the band, that all Zion was in an uproar.</u>**

32 Who immediately took soldiers and centurions, and **ran down unto them:** and <u>when they saw the chief captain and the soldiers, they left beating of Paul.</u>

Paul and the Jews that were out to kill him were outside the doors of the House of Yahweh, which sat below the Fort in the old part of the city of

Zion., verse 32 says they ran down to them, from the Fort, not down from the House of Yahweh, which they could not have done.

33 Then the chief captain came near, and took him, and commanded *him* to be bound with two chains; and demanded who he was, and what he had done.

34 And some cried one thing, some another, among the multitude: and when he could not know the certainty for the tumult, he commanded him to be carried into the castle.

Paul and the Jews that were out to kill him were outside the doors of the House of Yahweh, which sat below the Fort in the old part of the city of Zion., verse 32 says they ran down to them, from the Fort, not down from the House of Yahweh, which they could not have done. The Castle mentioned is speaking of **Fort Antonia, the fort of the Roman army. He came upon the stairs of the Fort**

35 **And when he came upon the stairs, so it was, that he was borne of the soldiers for the violence of the people.**

36 For the multitude of the people followed after, crying, Away with him.

37 And as Paul was to be led into the castle, he said unto the chief captain, May I speak unto thee? Who said, Canst thou speak Greek?

38 Art not thou that Egyptian, which before these days madest an uproar, and leddest out into the wilderness four thousand men that were murderers? **39** But Paul said, **I am a man *which am* a Jew of Tarsus, *a city* in Cilicia, a citizen of no mean city: and, I beseech thee, suffer me to speak unto the people.Paul stood upon the stairs leading up to the fort.**

40 And when he had given him licence, Paul stood on the stairs, and beckoned with the hand unto the people. And when there was made a great silence, he spake unto *them* in the Hebrew tongue, saying,

The following is Paul's speech explaining everything to the Jews and what happened afterward.

Acts 22: 1-30

1 Men, brethren, and fathers, **hear ye my defence *which I make* now unto you**.

2 (And **when they heard that he spake in the Hebrew tongue to them, they kept the more silence:** and he saith,)

3 I **am verily a man *which am* a Jew, born in Tarsus, *a city* in Cilicia, yet brought up in this city at the feet of Gamaliel, *and* taught according to the perfect manner of the law of the fathers, and was zealous toward Yahweh, as ye all are this day.**

4 And I persecuted this way unto the death, binding and delivering into prisons both men and women.

5 As also the high priest doth bear me witness, and all the estate of the elders: from whom also I received letters unto the brethren, and went to Damascus, to bring them which were there bound unto Zion, for to be punished.

6 And it came to pass, that, as I made my journey, and was come nigh unto Damascus about noon, suddenly there shone from heaven a great light round about me.

7 And I fell unto the ground, and heard a voice saying unto me, Saul, Saul, why persecutest thou me?

8 <u>And I answered, Who art thou, Master? And he said unto me, I am Yahweh, whom thou persecutest. 9And they that were with me saw indeed the light, and were afraid; but they heard not the voice of him that spake to me.</u>

10And I said, What shall I do, Master? And **Yahweh said unto me**, Arise, and go into Damascus; and there it shall be told thee of all things which are appointed for thee to do.

11And when I could not see for the righteousness of that light, being led by the hand of them that were with me, I came into Damascus.

12And one Ananias, a devout man according to the law, having a good report of all the Jews which dwelt *there*,

13Came unto me, and stood, and said unto me, Brother Saul, receive thy sight. And the same hour I looked up upon him.

14And he said, **Yahweh of our fathers hath chosen thee**, that thou shouldest know his will, and see that Just One, and shouldest hear the voice of his mouth.

15For thou shalt be his witness unto all men of what thou hast seen and heard.

16And now why tarriest thou? **arise, and be baptized, and wash away thy transgressions, calling on the name of Yahweh.**

17And it came to pass, that, when I was come again to Zion., even while I prayed in the House, I was in a trance;

18And saw him saying unto me, Make haste, and get thee quickly out of Zion: for they will not receive thy testimony concerning me.

19And I said, Lord, they know that I imprisoned and beat in every synagogue them that believed on thee:

20And when the blood of thy martyr Stephen was shed, I also was standing by, and consenting unto his death, and kept the raiment of them that slew him.

21And he said unto me, Depart: for I will send thee far hence unto the Gentiles.

22And they gave him audience unto this word, and *then* lifted up their voices, and said, Away with such a *fellow* from the earth: for it is not fit that he should live.

23And as they cried out, and cast off *their* clothes, and threw dust into the air,

24The chief captain commanded him to be brought into the castle, and bade that he should be examined by scourging; that he might know wherefore they cried so against him.

25And as they bound him with thongs, Paul said unto the centurion that stood by, Is it lawful for you to scourge a man that is a Roman, and uncondemned?

26When the centurion heard *that*, he went and told the chief captain, saying, Take heed what thou doest: for this man is a Roman.

27Then the chief captain came, and said unto him, Tell me, art thou a Roman? He said, Yea.

28And the chief captain answered, With a great sum obtained I this freedom. And Paul said, But I was *free* born.

29Then straightway they departed from him which should have examined him: and the chief captain also was afraid, after he knew that he was a Roman, and because he had bound him.

30On the morrow, because he would have known the certainty wherefore he was accused of the Jews, he loosed him from *his* bands, and commanded the chief priests and all their council to appear, and brought Paul down, and set him before them.

Acts 9:22-30

22 **But Saul increased the more in strength, and confounded the Jews which dwelt at Damascus, proving that this is very Yahweh.**

23 **And after that many days were fulfilled, the Jews took counsel to kill him:**

24 **But their laying await was known of Saul. And they watched the gates day and night to kill him.**

25 **Then the disciples took him by night, and let him down by the wall in a basket.**

26 **And when Saul was come to Zion, he assayed to join himself to the disciples: but they were all afraid of him, and believed not that he was a disciple.**

27 **But Barnabas took him, and brought him to the apostles, and declared unto them how he had seen Paul in the way, and that he had spoken to him, and how he had taught boldly at Damascus in the name of Yahweh.**

28 **And he was with them coming in and going out at Zion.**

29. **And he spake boldly in the name of Yahweh, and disputed against the Jews: but they went about to slay him.**

30 Which when the brethren knew, they brought him down to Caesarea, and sent him forth to Tarsus. 31 Then had the assemblies rest throughout all Judaea and Galilee and Samaria, and were edified; and walking in the fear of Yahweh, and in the comfort of the Spirit, were multiplied.

Acts 26:13-14

13 At midday, O king, I saw in the way a light from heaven, above the brightness of the sun, shining round about me and them which journeyed with me.

14 And when we were all fallen to the earth, I heard a voice speaking unto me, and saying in the Hebrew tongue, Saul, Saul, why persecutest thou me? it is hard for thee to kick against the pricks.

Acts 22:6,9,11

6. And it came to pass, that, as I made my journey, and was come nigh unto Damascus about noon, suddenly there shone from heaven a great light round about me.

9. And they that were with me saw indeed the light, and were afraid; but they heard not the voice of him that spake to me.

11. And when I could not see for the brilliance of that light, being led by the hand of them that were with me, I came into Damascus.

6A. THIS IS WHEN PAUL WAS GIVEN SALVATION, HE WAS A PERSECUTOR OF YAHWEH'S Jew Elect. Yahweh picked Paul to be an Apostle to the Gentiles. HE WAS SENT FIRST TO THE JEWS, THEY WOULD NOT ACCEPT HIM SO HE WAS LATER SENT TO THE GENTILES.

Acts 9: 22 But Saul increased the more in strength, and confounded the Jews which dwelt at Damascus, proving that this is very Yahweh.

Acts 9:7 And <u>the men which journeyed with him stood speechless, hearing a voice, but seeing no man.</u>

Notice in the above verse, "THEY HEARD A VOICE."

Acts 22:9. And they that were with me saw indeed the light, and were afraid; but they heard not the voice of him that spake to me.

Notice the above verse; PAUL SAID THAT, "THEY HEARD NOT THE VOICE."

Acts 9:1-31

1 And Saul, yet breathing out threatenings and slaughter against the disciples of Yahweh, went unto the high priest,

2 And desired of him letters to Damascus to the Jews, that if he found any of this way, whether they were men or women, he might bring them bound unto Zion.

Notice the above two verses show the mission of Paul and the men with him. What they were on their way to do. As you can see, someone lied. It wasn't Paul. Those men with him were to help him round up the believers in Yahweh, so they lied about hearing the voice. This was a spacecraft. It was about noon, and the light was even brighter than what the light of the sun was. The reason Paul had scales that fell off his eyes was the bright light burned his eyes. It was so bright.

Acts 9:18 And immediately there fell from his eyes as it had been scales: and he received sight forthwith, and arose, and was baptized.

You must read whole chapters to understand Paul and the Word that he taught came from Yahweh.

PAUL AND BARNABAS:

Acts 13:44-49 tells us that on a sabbath **[came almost the whole city together to hear the word of Yahweh]**. When the **Jews saw the multitudes, they were filled with envy** and spoke against the things which Paul said. Paul and Barnabas told them it was necessary that the word of Yahweh should first have been spoken to them, but **since they did not accept it, they turned to the Gentiles**. The Gentiles who heard this were glad and praised the word of Yahweh and **as many as were ordained to eternal life believed**. **[The word of Yahweh was published throughout the region]**.

Acts 13:50 tells us that *the Jews stirred up the devout and honorable women and the chief men of the city and raised persecution against Paul and Barnabas and kicked them out*.

Acts 14:1 tells us that **[Paul and Barnabas went together into the Synagogue of the Jews and spake]** that **a great multitude both of the Jews and of the Gentiles believed**.

Acts 14:3 tells us they stayed there a long time **[speaking boldly in Yahweh, giving testimony unto the word of his grace]** and *were granted signs and wonders to be done by their hands*.

Acts 14:5 tells us *they were going to be assaulted by Gentiles and Jews with their rulers to stone them,* but they were aware of this and fled.

ACTS 14:7 And there they preached the Word.

ACTS 14:8 And there sat a certain man at Lystra, impotent in his feet, being a cripple from his mother's womb, who never had walked:

ACTS 14:9 The same heard Paul speak: who stedfastly beholding him, and perceiving that he had faith to be healed,

ACTS 14:10 Said with a loud voice, Stand upright on thy feet. And he leaped and walked.

ACTS 14:16 Who in times past suffered all nations to walk in their own ways.

ACTS 14:19 And there came thither certain Jews from Antioch and Iconium, who persuaded the people, and having stoned Paul, drew him out of the city, supposing he had been dead.

ACTS 14:20 Howbeit, as the disciples stood round about him, he rose up, and came into the city: and the next day he departed with Barnabas to Derbe.

ACTS 14:21 And when they had taught the Word to that city, and had taught many, they returned again to Lystra, and to Iconium, and Antioch,

ACTS 14:22 Confirming the souls of the disciples, and exhorting them to continue in the faith, and that we must through much tribulation enter into the kingdom of Yahweh.

ACTS 14:23 And when they had ordained them elders in every assembly, and had prayed with fasting, they commended them to Yahweh, on whom they believed.

ACTS 14:25 And when they had taught the word in Perga, they went down into Attalia:

ACTS 14:27 And when they were come, and had gathered the assembly together, they rehearsed all that Yahweh had done with them, and how he had opened the door of faith unto the Gentiles.

Just from the book of Acts you can see just how many pagans were leaving paganism and coming to Yahweh. This made all the pagan kings and leaders angry, so they all came together to see how they could stop Yahweh's truth from spreading and silence His followers. This is proven by the following verses:

I'm going to go ahead and finish the book of Acts.

Acts 4:25-26

25: Who by the mouth of thy servant David hast said, Why did the heathen rage, and the people imagine vain things?

26: The Kings of the earth stood up and the rulers were gathered together against Yahweh and against his Messiah.

The following verse tells you why the heathen raged.

Acts 17:6 And when they found them not, they drew Jason and certain brethren unto the rulers of the city, crying, **These that have turned the world upside down are come hither also;**

THESE SIGNS SHALL FOLLOW THEM THAT BELIEVE: Yahweh working with them, and confirming the Word with signs following.

1.) **In my name shall they cast out Satan. - This was also proven throughout the scriptures.**

2.) **They shall speak with new tongues. - A tongue that could only come from Yahweh, tongues understood by all languages, why the true believers did not need an interpreter when they were sent to the ends of the earth to teach the Word.**

3.) **They shall take up serpents. - Paul proved this fact. Acts 28:3-6**

4.) If they drink any deadly thing, it shall not hurt them. - I believe they tried to kill true believers with poisons.

5.) They shall lay hands on the sick, and they shall (will) recover. - Not maybe, or might, but WILL, and they were, throughout the scriptures.

6.) They needed no man to teach them. The Spirit taught them all things. - No Spirit-filled person needed to go and listen to a teacher to teach them. They were teachers.

7.) They all knew that they would suffer persecution and would be killed.

Revelation 6:9

And when he had opened the fifth seal, **I saw under the table the souls of them that were slain for the word of Yahweh, and for the testimony which they held: As the future believers also will.**

Daniel 11:32

And such as do wickedly against the covenant shall he corrupt by flatteries: but the people that do know their Almighty shall be strong, and do *exploits.*

Galatians 1:1-24

1 Paul, an apostle, (not of men, neither by man, but by Yahweh Messiah, and Yahweh the Father, who raised him from the dead;)

2 And all the brethren which are with me, unto the assemblies of Galatia:

3 Peace *be* **to you and peace from Yahweh the Father, and** *from* **our Master Yahweh Messiah, 4 Who gave himself for our transgressions, that he might deliver us from this present evil world, according to the will of Yahweh and our Father:**

5 To whom *be* esteem for ever and ever.

6 I marvel that ye are so soon removed from him that called you into the Word of Yahweh unto another Word:

7 Which is not another; but **there be some that trouble you and would pervert the Word of Yahweh.**

8 But **though we, or a Messenger from heaven, teach any other Word unto you than that which we have taught unto you, let him be accursed.**

9 As we said before, so say I now again, **If any *man* teach any other Word unto you than that ye have received, let him be accursed.**

10 **For do I now persuade men, or Yahweh? or do I seek to please men? for if I yet pleased men, I should not be the servant of Yahweh.**

11 **But I certify you, brethren, that the Word which was taught of me is not after man.**

12 For **I neither received it of man, neither was I taught *it*, but by the revelation of Yahweh Messiah.**

13 For ye have heard of my conversation in time past in the Jews' faith, how that beyond measure **I persecuted the assemblies of Yahweh, and wasted it:**

14 And profited in the Jews' faith above many my equals in mine own nation, being more exceedingly zealous of the traditions of my fathers.

15 **But when it pleased Yahweh, who separated me from my mother's womb, and called *me* by his Spirit.**

16 **To reveal his Son in me, that I might teach him among the heathen; immediately I conferred not with flesh and blood:**

17 Neither went I up to Zion to them which were apostles before me; but I went into Arabia, and returned again unto Damascus.

18 Then after three years I went up to Zion to see Peter, and abode with him fifteen days.

19 But other of the apostles saw I none, save James Immanuel's brother.

20 **Now the things which I write unto you, behold, before Yahweh, I lie not**.

21 Afterwards I came into the regions of Syria and Cilicia;

22 And **was unknown by face unto the assemblies of Judaea which were in Yahweh:**

23 But **they had heard only, that he which persecuted us in times past now teaches the faith which once he destroyed.**

24 And **they praised Yahweh in me.**

1 Corinthians 9:1-27

<u>**1**</u> <u>**Am I not an apostle**</u>? am I not free? have I not seen Yahweh Messiah our Master? are not ye my work in Yahweh?

<u>**2**</u> **If I be not an apostle unto others,** <u>yet doubtless I am to you: for the seal of mine apostleship are ye in Yahweh.</u>

<u>**3**</u> **Mine answer to them that do examine me is this,**

<u>**4**</u> <u>Have we not power to eat and to drink?</u>

<u>**5**</u> <u>Have we not power to lead about a sister, a wife, as well as other apostles, and *as* the brethren of Yahweh, and Cephas?</u>

<u>**6**</u> **Or I only and Barnabas, have not we power to forbear working?**

<u>**7**</u> <u>Who goeth a warfare any time at his own charges? who planteth a vineyard, and eateth not of the fruit thereof? or who feedeth a flock, and eateth not of the milk of the flock?</u>

235

GARY WENDELL STANFIELD SR.

8 Say I these things as a man? or saith not the law the same also?

9 For it is written in the law of Moses, Thou shalt not muzzle the mouth of the ox that treadeth out the corn. Doth Yahweh take care for oxen?

10 Or saith he *it* altogether for our sakes? For our sakes, no doubt, *this* is written: that he that ploweth should plow in hope; and that he that thresheth in hope should be partaker of his hope.

11 **If we have sown unto you spiritual things, *is it* a great thing if we shall reap your carnal things?**

12 If others be partakers of *this* power over you, *are* not we rather? Nevertheless we have not used this power; but suffer all things, lest we should hinder the Word of Yahweh.

13 Do ye not know that they which minister/**TEACH** about **RIGHTEOUS** things live *of the things* of the **HOUSE OF YAHWEH**? and they which wait at the altar are partakers with the altar?

14 Even so hath **YAHWEH** ordained that they which preach/**TEACH** the gospel/**WORD** should live of the gospel/**WORD**.

15 But I have used none of these things: neither have I written these things, that it should be so done unto me: for *it were* better for me to die, than that any man should make my glorying/**ESTEEMING** void.

16 For though I preach/**TEACH** the gospel/**WORD**, I have nothing to glory/**ESTEEM** of; for necessity is laid upon me; yea, woe is unto me, if I preach/**TEACH** not the gospel/**WORD**!

17 For if I do this thing willingly, I have a reward: but if against my will, a dispensation *of the gospel/***WORD** is committed unto me.

236

18 What is my reward then? *Verily* that, when I preach/**TEACH** the gospel/**WORD**, I may make the gospel/WORD of Christ/**YAHWEH** without charge, that I abuse not my power in the gospel/**WORD**.

19 For though I be free from all *men*, yet have I made myself servant unto all, that I might gain the more.

20 And unto the Jews I became as a Jew, that I might gain the Jews; to them that are under the law, as under the law, that I might gain them that are under the law;

21 To them that are without law, as without law, (being not without law to God/**YAHWEH**, but under the law to Christ/**YAHWEH**,) that I might gain them that are without law.

22 To the weak became I as weak, that I might gain the weak: I am made all things to all *men*, that I might by all means save some.

23 And this I do for the gospel's/**WORD'S** sake, that I might be partaker thereof with *you*.

24 Know ye not that they which run in a race run all, but one receiveth the prize?

So run, that ye may obtain.

25 And every man that striveth for the mastery is temperate in all things.
Now they *do it* to obtain a corruptible crown; but we an incorruptible.

26 I therefore so run, not as uncertainly; so fight I, not as one that beateth the air:

27   But I keep under my body, and bring *it* into subjection: lest that by any means, when I have preached/**TAUGHT** to others, I myself should be a castaway.

1 Corinthian 2:1-16

1 **And I, brethren, when I came to you, came not with excellency of speech or of wisdom, declaring unto you the testimony of Yahweh**.

2 **For I determined not to know anything among you, save Yahweh Messiah, and him killed.**

3 And **I was with you in weakness,** and **in fear, and in much trembling.**

4 And **my speech and my teaching** *was* **not with enticing words of man's wisdom, but in demonstration of the Spirit and of power:**

5 **That your faith should not stand in the wisdom of men**, **but in the power of Yahweh.**

6 Howbeit **we speak wisdom among them that are perfect: yet not the wisdom of this world, nor of the Kings of this world, that come to nought:**

7 **But we speak the wisdom of Yahweh in a mystery,** *even* **the hidden** *wisdom***, which Yahweh ordained before the world unto our righteousness:** 8 **Which none of the princes of this world knew**: **for had they known** *it*, **they would not have killed Yahweh of righteousness.**

9But as it is written, Eye hath not seen, nor ear heard, neither have entered into the heart of man, **the things which Yahweh hath prepared for them that love him.**

10   But **Yahweh hath revealed** *them* **unto us by his Spirit**: for **the Spirit searcheth all things, yea, the deep things of Yahweh.**

11   For <u>what man knoweth the things of a man, save the spirit of man which is in him? even so the things of Yahweh knoweth no man,</u> **but the Spirit of Yahweh.**

12   Now <u>we have received, not the spirit of the world,</u> **but the spirit which is of Yahweh; that we might know the things that are freely given to us of Yahweh.**

13   **Which things also we speak**<u>, not in the words which man's wisdom teacheth,</u> **but which the Spirit teacheth; comparing spiritual things with spiritual.**

14   But <u>the natural man receiveth not the things of the Spirit of Yahweh: for they are foolishness unto him: neither can he know</u> *them*, **because they are spiritually discerned.**

15   But **he that is spiritual judgeth all things, yet he himself is judged of no man.**

16   For **who hath known the mind of Yahweh, that he may instruct him?**
But **we have the mind of Yahweh.**

Immanuel taught. He did no preaching like they do today; Paul and all the Apostles were teachers of Yahweh's Word, as were all the disciples, the very reason Immanuel was called Rabbi, which means teacher, not preacher. Preaching is a Christianity invention.

Ephesians 3:1-21

1 For this cause I Paul, the prisoner of Yahweh Messiah for you Gentiles,

2 If ye have heard of the dispensation of the Spirit of Yahweh which is given me to you-ward.

3 **How that by revelation he made known unto me the mystery; (as I wrote afore in few words,**

4 Whereby, **when ye read, ye may understand my knowledge in the mystery of Yahweh)**

5 Which <u>in other ages was not made known unto the sons of men</u>, as it is **now revealed unto his apostles and prophets by the Spirit;**

6 **That the Gentiles should be fellow heirs, and of the same body, and partakers of his promise in Yahweh by the Word:**

7 Whereof <u>**I was made a minister, according to the gift of the Spirit of Yahweh given unto me by the effectual working of his power.**</u>

8 <u>**Unto me, who am less than the least of all Elect,**</u> **is this Spirit given, that I should teach among the Gentiles the unsearchable riches of Yahweh;**

9 And **to make all** *men* **see what** *is* **the fellowship of the mystery, which from the beginning of the world hath been hid in Yahweh, who created all things by Yahweh Messiah:**

10 **To the intent that now unto the principalities and powers in heavenly** *places* **might be known by the Elect the manifold wisdom of Yahweh,**

11 **According to the eternal purpose which he purposed in Yahweh Messiah our Master:**

12 **In whom we have boldness and access with confidence by the faith of him.**

13 Wherefore **I desire that ye faint not at my tribulations for you, which is your righteousness.**

14   For this cause I bow my knees unto the Father of our Master Yahweh Messiah,

15   Of whom the whole family in heaven and earth is named,

16   That he would grant you, according to the riches of his righteousness, to be strengthened with might by his Spirit in the inner man;

17   That Yahweh may dwell in your hearts by faith; that ye, being rooted and grounded in love,

18   May be able to comprehend with all Elect what *is* the breadth, and length, and depth, and height;

19   And to know the love of Yahweh, which passeth knowledge, that ye might be filled with all the fulness of Yahweh.

20   Now unto him that is able to do exceeding abundantly above all that we ask or think, according to the power that worketh in us,

21   Unto him *be* righteousness in the assemblies by Messiah Yahweh throughout all ages, world without end.

7A. ACTS 19:1-41 PROVES OVER AND OVER THAT PAUL WAS A TRUE APOSTLE

1 And it came to pass, that, while Apollos was at Corinth, **Paul having passed through the upper coasts came to Ephesus: and finding certain disciples,**

2 He said unto them, **Have ye received the Spirit since ye believed?** And they said unto him, **We have not so much as heard whether there be any Spirit.**

3 And he said unto them, Unto what then were ye baptized? And they said, Unto John's baptism.

4 Then said Paul, **John verily baptized with the baptism of repentance, saying unto the people, that they should believe on him which should come after him, that is, on Messiah Yahweh.**

5 When they heard *this,* **they were baptized in the name of Yahweh.**

6 And when Paul had laid *his* hands upon them, **the Spirit came on them; and they spake with tongues, and prophesied.**

7 And all the men were about twelve.

8And he went into the **city,** and **spake boldly for the space of three months**, **disputing and persuading** **the things concerning the kingdom of Yahweh.**

9 But when divers were hardened, and believed not, but spake evil of that way before the multitude, he departed from them, and **separated the disciples, disputing daily in the school of one Tyrannus**.

10 And this continued by the space of two years; **so that all they which dwelt in Asia heard the word of Yahweh, both Jews and Gentiles.**

11 **And Yahweh wrought special miracles by the hands of Paul:**

12 **So that from his body were brought unto the sick handkerchiefs or aprons, and the diseases departed from them, and the evil spirits went out of them.**

13 Then certain of the vagabond Jews, exorcists, took upon them to call over them which had evil spirits the name of **Yahweh, saying, We adjure you by Yahweh whom Paul teacheth.**

14 And there were seven sons of *one* Sceva, a Jew, *and* chief of the priests, which did so.

15   And the evil spirit answered and said, **Yahweh I know, and Paul I know; but who are ye?**

16   And the man in whom the evil spirit was leaped on them, and overcame them, and prevailed against them, so that they fled out of that house naked and wounded.

17   And this was known to all the Jews and Greeks also dwelling at Ephesus; and fear fell on them all, and **the name of Yahweh was magnified.**

This Chapter alone proves that Paul was an Apostle of Yahweh by people being filled with the Spirit with his laying on of hands and the special miracles with healings from handkerchiefs and aprons and the evil spirits saying they knew who Yahweh and Paul were, so all you anti-Paul people can learn a good lesson from this whole study but especially just by this chapter.

18   And many that believed came, and confessed, and shewed their deeds.

19   **Many of them also which used curious arts brought their books together, and burned them before all** *men:* and they counted the price of them, and found *it* fifty thousand *pieces* of silver.

20   So **mightily grew the Word of Yahweh and prevailed.**

21   After these things were ended, **Paul purposed in the spirit, when he had passed through Macedonia and Achaia, to go to Zion, saying, After I have been there, I must also see Rome.**

22   So he sent into Macedonia two of them that ministered unto him, Timotheus and Erastus; but **he himself stayed in Asia for a season.**

23   And the same time there arose no small stir about that way.

24   For a certain *man* named Demetrius, a silversmith, which made silver shrines for Diana, brought no small gain unto the craftsmen;

25   Whom he called together with the workmen of like occupation, and said, Sirs, ye know that by this craft we have our wealth.

26   Moreover ye see and hear, that not alone at Ephesus, but almost throughout all Asia, **this Paul hath persuaded and turned away much people, saying that they be no gods, which are made with hands**

27   So that not only this our craft is in danger to be set at nought; but also that the temple of the great goddess Diana should be despised, and her magnificence should be destroyed, whom all Asia and the world worshippeth.

Acts 19:35:

35 After quieting the crowd, the town clerk *said, "Men of Ephesus, what man is there after all who does not know that the city of the **Ephesians is guardian of the temple of the great Artemis [Diana]** and of the *image* which fell down from heaven?

<u>Dianna is another name for Semiramis in her worship.</u>

28   And when they heard *these sayings*, they were full of wrath, and cried out, saying, Great *is* Diana of the Ephesians.

29   And the whole city was filled with confusion: and having caught Gaius and Aristarchus, men of Macedonia, Paul's companions in travel, they rushed with one accord into the theatre.

30   And **when Paul would have entered in unto the people, the disciples suffered him not.**

31   And **certain of the chief of Asia, which were his friends, sent unto him, desiring** *him* **that he would not adventure himself into the theatre.**

32   Some therefore cried one thing, and some another: <u>for the assembly was confused; and the more part knew not wherefore they were come together.</u>

33   And they drew Alexander out of the multitude, the Jews putting him forward. And Alexander beckoned with the hand, and would have made his defence unto the people.

34   But **when they knew that he was a Jew, all with one voice about the space of two hours cried out, Great** *is* **Diana of the Ephesians.**

35   **And when the town clerk had appeased the people, he said,** *Ye* **men of Ephesus, what man is there that knoweth not how that the city of the Ephesians is a worshiper of the great goddess Diana, and of the** *image* **which fell down from Jupiter?**

36   Seeing then that these things cannot be spoken against, ye ought to be quiet, and to do nothing rashly.

37   <u>For ye have brought hither these men, which are neither robbers of churches, nor yet blasphemers of your goddess.</u>

38   <u>Wherefore if Demetrius, and the craftsmen which are with him, have a matter against any man, the law is open, and there are deputies: let them implead one another.</u>

39   <u>But if ye enquire any thing concerning other matters, it shall be determined in a lawful assembly.</u>

40   <u>For we are in danger to be called in question for this day's uproar, there being no cause whereby we may give an account of this concourse.</u>

41   <u>And when he had thus spoken, he dismissed the assembly.</u>

PAUL'S COLLECTIONS FOR THE ELECT WHO WERE FACING FAMINE: THIS HAD NOTHING TO DO WITH TITHING OR THE SABBATH BEING THE FIRST DAY OF THE WEEK.

Collection for the Elect going without and Paul was collecting it to take to them.

Another scripture that preachers use for tithing has nothing to do with tithing. I'll prove how it fits in with its own context of scriptures. They even use these to try and prove a Sunday Sabbath, saying Paul met on the first day of the week.

This is the scripture they use:

1 Cor. 16:1-2

1: Now concerning the collection for the elect, as I have given order to the assemblies of Galatia, even so do ye.

2: Upon the first day of the week let every one of you lay by him in store, as Yahweh hath prospered him, that there be no gatherings when I come.

Let's see what Paul is actually talking about here and also putting the above scripture in the context where it rightfully belongs.

Acts 11:27-30

27: And in these days came prophets from Zion unto Antioch.

28: And there stood up one of them named Agabus, and signified by the Spirit that there should be great dearth throughout all the world: which came to pass in the days of Claudius Caesar.

29: Then the disciples, every man according to his ability, determined to send relief unto the brethren which dwelt in Judaea:

30: Which also they did, and sent it to the elders by the hands of Barnabas and Saul.

1 Cor. 16:1-5

1: Now concerning the collection for the elect, as I have given order to the assemblies of Galatia, even so do ye.

2: Upon the first day of the week let every one of you lay by him in store, as Yahweh hath prospered him, that there be no gatherings when I come.

3: And when I come, whomsoever ye shall approve by your letters, them will I send to bring your liberality unto Zion.

4: And if it be meet that I go also, they shall go with me.

5: Now I will come unto you, when I shall pass through Macedonia: for I do pass through Macedonia.

2 Cor. 8:1-24

1: Moreover, brethren, we do you to wit of the Spirit of Yahweh bestowed on the assemblies of Macedonia;

2: How that in a great trial of affliction the abundance of their joy and their deep poverty abounded unto the riches of the liberality.

247

3: For to their power, I bear record, yea, and beyond their power they were willing of themselves; 4: Praying us with much entreaty that we would receive the gift, and take upon us the fellowship of the ministering to the elect.

5: And this they did, not as we hoped, but first gave their own selves to Yahweh, and unto us by the will of Yahweh.

6: Insomuch that we desired Titus, that as he had begun so he would also finish in you the same ministry also.

7: Therefore, as ye abound in everything, in faith, and utterance, and knowledge, and in all diligence, and in your love to us, see that ye abound in this ministry too.

8: I speak not by commandment, but by occasion of the forwardness of others, and to prove the sincerity of your love.

9: For ye know the love of our Master, Yahweh the Messiah, that, though he was rich, yet for your sakes he became poor, that ye through his poverty might be rich.

10: And herein I give my advice: for this is expedient for you, who have begun before, not only to do, but also to be forward a year ago.

11: Now therefore perform the doing of it; that as there was a readiness to will, so there may be a performance also out of that which ye have

12: For if there be first a willing mind, it is accepted according to that a man hath, and not according tot hat he hath not.

13: For I mean not that other men be eased, and ye burdened:

14: But by an equality, that now at this time your abundance may be a supply for their want, that their abundance also may be a supply for your want: that there may be equality

15: As it is written, He that had gathered much had nothing over; and he that had gathered little had no lack. < love that verse.

16: But thanks be to Yahweh, which put the same earnest care into the heart of Titus for you.

17: For indeed he accepted the exhortation; but being more forward, of his own accord he went unto you.

18: And we have sent with him the brother, whose praise is in the word throughout all the assemblies;

19: And not that only, but who was also chosen of the assemblies to travel with us with this offering, which is administered by us to the honor of Yahweh, and declaration of your ready mind:

20: Avoiding this, that no man should blame us in this abundance which is administered by us:

21: Providing for honest things, not only in the sight of Yahweh, but also in the sight of men.

22: And we have sent with them our brother, whom we have often times proved diligent in many things, but now much more diligent, upon the great confidence which I have in you.

23: Whether any do enquire of Titus, he is my partner and fellow helper concerning you: or our brethren be enquired of, they are the messengers of the assemblies, and the servants of Yahweh.

24: Wherefore show ye to them, and before the assemblies, the proof of your love, and of our boasting on your behalf.

WOMEN HEAD COVERINGS:

1 Corinthians chapter 11:4-15

4 Every man praying or prophesying, having his head covered, dishonoureth his head.

+++HAVING LONG HAIR+++

5 But every woman that prayeth or prophesieth with her head uncovered dishonoureth her head: for that is even all one as if she were shaven.

+++ HAVING SHORT HAIR +++

6 For if the woman be not covered, let her also be shorn: but if it be a shame for a woman to be shorn or shaven, let her be covered.

+++ HAVING LONG HAIR +++ a woman who prayed or prophesied with her head uncovered it was the equivalent to her head being shaven.+++

7 For a man indeed ought not to cover his head, forasmuch as he is the image and esteem of Yahweh: but the woman is the esteem of the man.

+++ HAVE LONG HAIR +++

8 For the man is not of the woman; but the woman of the man.

9 Neither was the man created for the woman; but the woman for the man.

10 For this cause ought the woman to have power on her head because of the Messengers.

+++ MEN WERE TRYING TO USURP AUTHORITY OVER THE WOMAN +++

11 Nevertheless neither is the man without the woman, neither the woman without the man, in Yahweh.

12 For as the woman is of the man, even so is the man also by the woman; but all things of Yahweh.

13 Judge in yourselves: is it comely that a woman pray unto YAHWEH uncovered?

+++ WITH SHORT HAIR +++

14 Doth not even nature itself teach you, that, IF A MAN HAVE LONG HAIR, IT IS A SHAME TO HIM?

15 But if a woman have long hair, it is a esteem to her: FOR HER HAIR IS GIVEN HER FOR A COVERING.

+++ THIS VERSE 15 SAYS IT ALL +++

16 But if any man seem to be contentious, we have no such teaching, neither the assemblies of Yahweh.

BECAUSE THEY BELIEVED WOMEN SHOULD HAVE A HEAD COVERING TO WEAR. This was and is a man-made belief.

Let your women keep silent in the assemblies, for they have no permission to teach but to be in subjection.

1 Corinthians 14:6

6. Now, brethren, if I come unto you speaking with tongues, what shall I profit you, except I shall speak to you either by revelation, or by knowledge, or by PROPHECYING, or by doctrine?

1 Corinthians 11:6 For if the woman be not covered, let her also be shorn: but if it be a shame for a woman to be shorn or shaven, let her be covered.

+++ **HAVING LONG HAIR** +++ A woman who prayed or PROPHESIED with her head uncovered it was the equivalent of her head being shaven.+++

1 Corinthians 14:23 If therefore the whole assembly be come together into one place, and all speak with tongues, and there come in those that are unlearned, or unbelievers, will they not say that ye are mad?

Scriptures prove you must have Yahweh's Spirit infilling to be His. Men and Women alike. They all had the gifts of the Spirit, Men and Women. They did what the Spirit had them to do, Men and Women. They took the Word to the world doing miracles and healings with Yahweh working with them, male and female alike.

1 Corinthians 14:34-40

34. Let your women keep silence in the assemblies: for it is not permitted unto them to speak; but they are commanded to be under obedience, as also saith the law.

35. And if they will learn any thing, let them ask their husbands at home: for it is a shame for women to speak in the assembly.

36. WHAT? came the word of Yahweh out from you? or came it unto you only?

37. If any man think himself to be a prophet, or spiritual, let him acknowledge that the things that I write unto you are the commandments of Yahweh.

38. But if any man be ignorant, let him be ignorant.

^{39.} Wherefore, brethren, covet to prophesy, and forbid not to speak with tongues.

^{40.} Let all things be done decently and in order.

Galatians 3:28 There is neither Jew nor Greek, there is neither bond nor free, there is neither male nor female: for ye are all one in Messiah Yahweh.

CHAPTER 30

THESE SIGNS SHALL FOLLOW THEM:

Mark 16:20 And they went forth, and taught everywhere, Yahweh working with them, and confirming the word with signs following.

1.) In my name shall they cast out demons. - This was also proven throughout scriptures.

2.) They shall speak with new tongues. - A tongue that could only come from Yahweh, tongues understood by all languages, why the true believers did not need an interpreter when they were sent to the ends of the earth to preach the Word.

3.) They shall take up serpents. - Paul proved this fact. Acts 28:3-6

4.) If they drink any deadly thing, it shall not hurt them. - I believe they tried to kill true believers with poisons.

5.) They shall lay hands on the sick and they shall (will) recover. - Not maybe, or might, but WILL and they were, throughout the scriptures.

6.) They needed no man to teach them, the Spirit taught them all things. No Spirit filled person needed to go and listen to a teacher to teach them, they were teachers.

1 Corinthians 1:11 For it hath been declared unto me of you, my brethren, by THEM WHICH ARE OF THE HOUSE OF CHLOE, that there are contentions among you.

Colossians 4:15 Give my greetings to the brothers at Laodicea, and to Nympha and the assembly that MEETS AT HER HOUSE.

Acts 8:3 But <u>Saul began to destroy the assembly. Going from house to house</u>, he <u>dragged off men and women and put them in prison.</u>

Let your women keep silent in the assemblies??? I don't think so!!!!!!!!

Matthew 18:20

"For where two or three are gathered together in my name, there am I in the midst of them."

Does not matter if there are two or three women, one woman and two men; one man and two women, three men, or what have you.

John 14:26 <u>But the Helper, the Spirit, whom the Father will send in My name, He will teach you all things, and bring to your remembrance all that I said to you.</u>

Nehemiah 9:20 "<u>You gave Your good Spirit to instruct them, Your</u> manna You did not withhold from their mouth, And You gave them water for their thirst.

Matthew 10:19-20

<u>**But when they hand you over, do not worry about how or what you are to say; for it will be given** to you in that hour what you are to say. **For it is not you who speak, but it is the Spirit of your Father who speaks in you.**</u>

Mark 13:11 When they arrest you and hand you over, do not worry beforehand about what you are to say, **<u>but say whatever is given you in that hour; for it is not you who speak, but it is the Spirit.</u>**

Luke 12:12 <u>For the Spirit will teach you in that very hour what you ought to say.</u>

<u>1 John 2:27</u>

<u>As for you, the anointing which you received from Him abides in you, and you have no need for anyone to teach you; but as His anointing teaches you about all things, and is true and is not a lie, and just as it has taught you, you abide in Him.</u>

The Spirit-filled taught the ones that were not Spirit-filled yet back then to make them stronger in their faith until Yahweh filled them with his Spirit.

Matthew 23:8-12

8 But be not ye called Rabbi: for one is your Master, even Yahweh; and all ye are brethren.

9 And call no man your father upon the earth: for one is your Father, which is in heaven.

10 Neither <u>be ye called masters: for one is your Master, even Yahweh.</u>

From all the translations below are translations that used a different word for Master means: 4/Instructor, 5/Leader, 5/Teacher, 1/Guide, 1/Director,

English Standard Version

10 Neither be called instructors, for you have one **instructor**, the Christ.

New American Standard Bible

10 Do not be called leaders; for One is your **Leader**, that is, Christ.

New International Version

10 Nor are you to be called instructors, for you have one **Instructo**r, the Messiah.

New King James Version

¹⁰ And do not be called teachers; for One is your **Teacher**, the Christ.

New Living Translation

¹⁰ And don't let anyone call you 'Teacher,' for you have only one **teacher**, the Messiah. **New Revised Standard**

¹⁰ Nor are you to be called instructors, for you have one **instructor**, the Messiah.

The Bible in Basic English

¹⁰ And you may not be named guides: because one is your **Guide**, even Christ.

Common English Bible

¹⁰ Don't be called teacher because Christ is your one **teacher**.

Common English Bible w/ Apocrypha

¹⁰ Don't be called teacher because Christ is your one **teacher**.

The Complete Jewish Bible

¹⁰ Nor are you to let yourselves be called `leaders' because you have one **Leader**, and he is the Messiah!

The Darby Translation

10 Neither be called instructors, for one is your **instructor**, the Christ.

Good News Translation

10 Nor should you be called "Leader,' because your one and only **leader** is the Messiah.

GOD'S WORD Translation

10 Don't make others call you a leader because you have only one **leader**, the Messiah.

Lexham English Bible

10 And do not be called teachers, because one is your **teacher**, the Christ.

New International Reader's Version

10 You shouldn't be called 'teacher.' You have one **Teacher**, and he is the Christ.

New Revised Standard w/ Apocrypha

10 Nor are you to be called instructors, for you have one **instructor**, the Messiah.

Weymouth New Testament

10 And do not accept the name of `leader,' for your **Leader** is one alone-the Christ.

Young's Literal Translation

10nor may ye be called directors, for one is your **director** -- the Christ.

11But he that is greatest among you shall be your servant.

12And whosoever shall exalt himself shall be abased; and he that shall humble himself shall be exalt.

THE DECEITFUL TREE

There was a tree that started growing from its unaltered roots. As it grew, it started to become a majestic oak, but something happened. As the branches started to grow from their trunk, new branches were grafted to take their place. Branches from an apple, evergreen, maple, fig, walnut tree, and so on. As the tree grew, new branches were grafted in. As these branches took hold, the tree started growing its own smaller branches from these. Finally, when it was fully grown, it looked like a tree that no one had ever seen before. The tree appealed to all humanity. All the grafting on this tree concealed the original kind of tree it was. The name that was picked for this new-looking tree was Christianity.

By Gary W. Stanfield

CHAPTER 31

APOSTLE CREED

The term Christianity did not appear until the 4th century under Constantine being sold as truth, even though it was a pagan religion. So, it came from Constantine and why he propagandized the "Word of Yahweh" and put it in Greek from the original Hebrew and propagandized, and Jerome put them in Latin; Jerome's Latin Vulgate.

The 4th-century Constantine's so-called "Apostles' Creed" states belief in the communion of Saints, which certain Christian churches interpret as supporting the intercession of Saints.

325 C.E., Original Constantine's Nicene Creed at Council of Nicaea. The Word "creed" comes from the Latin word "credo," which means "I believe." It has been added to and changed since this one.

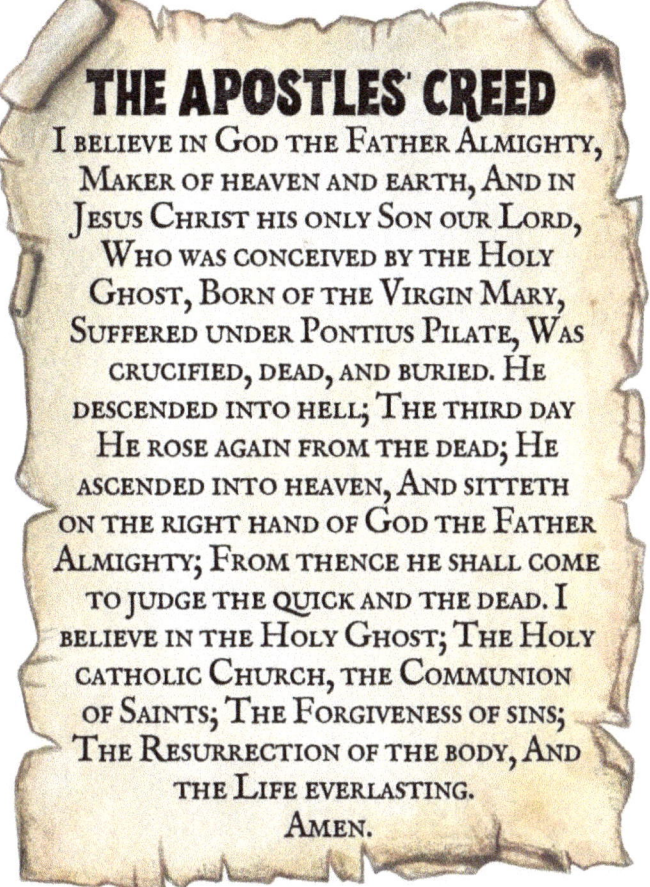

Words from the Creed: God, Jesus, Christ, Lord, and Amen are all sun deity names, and Constantine was a sun worshiper.

Hell is also a sun deity name and a pagan deity of the Underworld or dead. There is no such thing as a

Holy Ghost;

"HOLY" is derived from the divinely honored sun.

Holy, Holiday, and Holy Spirit are all interrelated and come from the Hindu religion. The words are derived from "Holi," which is the great Hindu spring festival held in honor of "Krishna," the Hindu Sun-deity. "GHOST" is an apparition. There is no such thing. Yahweh is Spirit, and the scriptures state, "No man has seen the Father." Just for that reason, the Son says,

"**When you have seen me, you have seen the Father. He is the Flesh of the Father. Conceived by the Holy Ghost?**

Colossians 1:15

15. Who is the IMAGE OF THE INVISIBLE YAHWEH, the firstborn of all creation;

Yahweh planted Joseph's seed in Mariam without her ever having a sexual relationship with Joseph. Immanuel was Joseph's biological son, just like the rest of Joseph's and Mariam's children. Yahweh used Immanuel for his purpose and, through the Spirit, raised him to do his will without any transgressions. To become the flesh of His Spirit fully. Yahweh took on the Flesh to become the offered Lamb. Immanuel became Yahweh's Messiah, the Father in the Flesh.

Immanuel was not crucified. He was beaten to within an inch of his life, then hung by his wrists with rope from an Olive tree, until he gave up the Spirit and died. When he said,"*"Eli, Eli, lema sabachthani?* "*I believe that he felt the Spirit leaving him because Yahweh had to take His Spirit so the flesh could die.*

MATTHEW 27:46

"And about the ninth hour Immanuel cried with a loud voice, saying, Eli, Eli, lama sabachthani? That is to say, My God, my God, why hast thou forsaken me?"

IMMANUEL WOULD NEVER HAVE USED THE WORD "GOD". HE WOULD HAVE SAID, MY אב (AB) FATHER, MY אב (AB) FATHER, WHY HAS THOU FORSAKEN ME?

HOW DID HE TEACH THEM TO PRAY?

THE "OUR FATHER" PRAYER

OUR FATHER WHICH ART IN HEAVEN,

RIGHTEOUS BE THY NAME

THY KINGDOM COME THY WILL BE DONE IN EARTH AS IT IS IN HEAVEN. ETC.

HE DID NOT SAY, OUR GOD WHICH ART IN HEAVEN!

IN THE Garden of Gethsemane, HE PRAYED TO THE FATHER!

Matthew 26:39,42

[39] After walking a little farther, he quickly bowed with his face to the ground and prayed, "**Father,** if it's possible, let this cup of suffering be taken away from me. But let your will be done rather than mine."

[42] Then he went away a second time and prayed, "**Father**, if this cup cannot be taken away unless I drink it, let your will be done."

WHAT HE TOLD HIS MOTHER:

Luke 2:49:

And he said unto them, How is it that ye sought me? Wist ye not that I must be about my **Father's** business?

John 5:43: I come in my **Father's** name, and ye receive me not: if another shall come in his own name, him ye will receive.

John 14:9: Anyone who has seen Me has seen the Father.

John 10:30: I and the **Father** are one.

Revelation 3:12

Him that overcometh will I make a pillar in the House of my **Father**, and he shall go no more out: and I will write upon him the name of my Father, and the name of the city of my **Father**, which is new Zion, which cometh down out of heaven from my **Father**: and I will write upon him my new name.

THESE VERSES SHOULD PROVE THAT IMMANUEL ALWAYS CALLED YAHWEH, FATHER.

The Holy Catholic Church; Constantine used the word Catholic for his Christian religion, which means Universal. "CHURCH" can only be found in Wycliff's translation when speaking of a pagan temple.

CIRCE was a Greek female deity pronounced Kirke'

Scottish, it is Kirk,

In German, it is Kirche

Netherlands, it is Kerk for the word church.

Anglo-Saxon root Circe, daughter of Helios, the Sun-deity; Tyndale used the word "CHURCHES" in his translation only in one place in Acts where it spoke of pagan temples.

Ekklesia = Greek for assembly or congregation,

The proper terminology to be used as the meeting place after the House of Yahweh was destroyed is "House." Those that met in people's homes were called assemblies.

Communion of Saints,

"SAINT"

The proper word to use is "upright" or "Elect" in place of Saint since the scriptures tell us the following in Romans:

Romans 3:10 As it is written, There is none righteous, no, not one

The etymology of the word "saint" – its origin and meaning: It came into use in the English language around the 1100s as an adjective used for those whom the Catholic Church had "beatified" and "canonized." At that time, the meaning of the word "saint" was "holy," corresponding to the Latin adjective *sanctus*, which meant "holy" and "sacred" (related to the verb *sancio*, "to consecrate"). So, in the 1100s, "saint Eligius" simply meant "holy Eligius." Later, in the

In the 1300s or so, the word "saint" began to be used even as a noun, "a saint," but it still referred to the

Catholic "saints" were not used for living persons.

The word Sacred is a sun deity name. , Holy is derived from the divinely honored sun. So it seems that since it did come from Rome, that Saint has something to do with the sun and sun worship.

This is how the English word "saint" came into being:

• The Greek (Erasmus) text of the New Testament has *hagios* (ἅγιος).
Jerome's Latin Vulgate version translated that into Latin as *Sanctus*.

• Wycliffe, whose 1395 English translation was based on (Jerome's) Latin text and not on Greek, did not translate the Latin *sanctus* but used it in the transcribed form "seyntis."

• Later, the spelling was changed further to "sainctes" (Tyndale, 1525), "sayntes" (Coverdale, 1535), "saintes" (Geneva bible, 1560), and finally, "saints" (Geneva Bible, 1587). "SIN" is a Moon deity, just like the Muslim deity ALLAH. Many scholars have also noticed that the moon-deity's name, *Sín*, is a part of such Arabic words as "Sinai," the "wilderness of Sîn," and so forth.

A scene from the time of Abraham. A merchant, his wife, and daughter at the ziggurat of Ur, prayerfully watching parading

priests and musicians restore a gilded statue of the moon god Sîn to his temple atop the "Hill of Heaven."

This comes from the Sumerian moon god Zeun or Suen. The King of the (lunar) disk, who sheds light.

"[The Sumerian god] Sin was represented in human form with a thin crescent above his head, presaging the halos of medieval saints." Ibid., p. 126

The proper terminology to be used is "transgression."

CHAPTER 32

THE FAITH IN YAHWEH HAS NOTHING TO DO WITH PAGAN CHRISTIANITY!

THE LATEST WORDS THAT I FOUND THAT WERE SWITCHED TO TEACH LIES: CITY / CITIES – TRUTH / SYNAGOGUE – SYNAGOGUES – THE LIE

THERE ARE AT LEAST 30 VERSES WITH SYNAGOGUE OR SYNAGOGUES, WHICH REPLACED CITY OR CITIES WITH SYNAGOGUES USED BY MOON WORSHIPERS. LOOK UP A FEW THAT I DON'T HAVE BELOW AND PROVE IT FOR YOURSELF.

Acts 6:9 "Then there arose certain of the synagogue/**city**, which is called the synagogue/city of the Libertines, and Cyrenians, and Alexandrians, and of them of Cilicia and of Asia, disputing with Stephen."

John 6:59 These things said he in the synagogue/**city**, as he taught in Capernaum.

Luke 7:5 For he loveth our nation, and he hath built us a synagogue/**city**.

Matthew 12:9 And when he was departed thence, he went into their synagogue/**city**:

Mark 1:23 "And there was in their synagogue/**city** a man with an **unclean spirit**; and he cried out,"

Luke 4:28 "And all they in the synagogue/**city**, when they heard these things, were filled with wrath,"

Acts 17:1 Now when they had passed through Amphipolis and Apollonia, they came to Thessalonica, where was a <u>synagogue/**city**</u> of the Jews:

Mark 1:21 And they went into **Capernaum**; and straightway on the sabbath day he entered into the synagogue<u>/**city**</u> and taught.

Luke 4:20 And he closed the book, and he gave it again to the minister/**RABBI/TEACHER**, and sat down. And the eyes of all them that were in the synagogue/**city** were fastened on him.

Luke 4:44 And he preached in the <u>synagogues/CITIES</u> of Galilee.

<u>THE ONLY VERSE THAT THIS DOES NOT WORK OUT IN   IS REVELATION 3:9</u> Behold, I will make them of the **synagogue / ASSEMBLY** of Satan, which say they are Jews, and are not, but do lie; behold, I will make them to come and worship before thy feet, and to know that I have loved thee.

Which would be Assembly and not Synagogue.

Teach / teaching/ taught – THE TRUTH - preach/ preaching/preached - THE LIE

It all has to do with teaching and not preaching.

WORD - THE TRUTH / GOSPEL – THE LIE

<u>**Mark 16:15**</u> - And he said unto them, Go ye into all the world, and preach/**TEACH** the gospel/**WORD** to every creature.

SPIRIT – THE TRUTH / HOLY GHOST - THE LIE

1 Corinthians 2:13 - Which things also we speak, not in the words which man's wisdom teaches, but which the Holy Ghost/**SPIRIT** teaches; comparing spiritual things with spiritual.

PASSOVER – THE TRUTH / EASTER – THE LIE

Acts 12:4 And when he had apprehended him, he put him in prison, and delivered him to four quaternions of soldiers to keep him; intending after Easter/**PASSOVER** to bring him forth to the people.

OFFER – THE TRUTH / SACRIFICE – THE LIE

Mark 14:12 On the first day of the Festival of Unleavened Bread, when it was customary to **sacrifice/OFFER** the Passover lamb, Immanuel's disciples asked him, "Where do you want us to go and make preparations for you to eat the Passover?"

LETTER – THE TRUTH / EPISTLE – THE LIE

2 Corinthians 3:1

Do we begin again to commend ourselves? or need we, as some others, epistles of commendation to you, or letters of commendation from you?

2 Peter 3:16

As also in all his epistles/**LETTERS**, speaking in them of these things; in which are some things hard to be understood, which they that are unlearned and unstable wrest, as they do also the other scriptures, unto their own destruction.

Romans 16:22

I Tertius, who wrote this epistle/**LETTER**, salute you in <u>the Lord</u>/**YAHWEH**.

The word "epistle" comes from the Greek word epistolé, *AND LATIN IS epistola*, which means "letter," "message," or "dispatch." In Hebrew, the word is *iggerah*, also meaning "letter". From the Hebrew, it should be letter.

2 Thess. 2:15 Therefore, brethren, stand fast, and hold the tradition / TEACHING which ye have been taught, whether by word, or our epistle/LETTER.

THE WORD OF YAHWEH WAS IN HEBREW; CONSTANTINE PUT IT IN GREEK, SO TO MAKE IT LOOK LIKE THE WORD OF YAHWEH WAS ORIGINALLY IN GREEK, THEY CAME UP WITH USING GREEK WORDS INSTEAD OF HEBREW WORDS OVER TO ENGLISH. THIS WAY PEOPLE WILL BELIEVE THE ORIGINAL GREEK LIE.

2 Thess. 2:15 Therefore, brethren, stand fast, and hold the tradition/TEACHING which ye have been taught, whether by word, or our epistle/LETTER.

OVER 44,000 DENOMINATIONS IN CHRISTIANITY

ONLY ONE FAITH IN YAHWEH

THINK ABOUT THIS TODAY: THEY SAY THAT THE UNITED STATES IS 65 PERCENT CHRISTIAN, AND THE PERCENTAGE RATE GOES HIGHER THE FARTHER BACK IN TIME THAT YOU GO. THIS CHRISTIAN NATION HAS LEGALIZED DRINKING, GAMBLING, ABORTION, HOMOSEXUALITY, DOPE, AND IN SOME PLACES EVEN PROSTITUTION. THIS SHOULD PROVE BEYOND A DOUBT THAT CHRISTIANITY IS OF SATAN.

BRAINWASHED

"When your mind has been programmed to believe certain things, your mind is also programmed to reject anything that teaches against them."

Gary W. Stanfield